I0168097

# Evita's True Story

*Since I Was Saved: 1981/2*

Written By Yvonne Woods 1991:
To Be Published. 2020.

By Author Evita Cleverly.

Grosvenor House
Publishing Limited

This book is published by
Grosvenor House Publishing Ltd
Link House
140 The Broadway, Tolworth, Surrey, KT6 7HT.
www.grosvenorhousepublishing.co.uk

A CIP record for this book
is available from the British Library

ISBN 978-1-83975-563-7

Hallelujah, it's me, Evita (my nickname, as I was christened Yvonne Elizabeth) back again.

It was 1981/2 when I first put pen to paper, recalling my absolute blessings and miraculous happenings 39 years ago. Now I realise how many years have gone by, so much more has happened in my life, and we are now in the year of the Covid-19 virus pandemic, 2020.

I have received absolute inspiration from my Heavenly Father, as I can honestly say that never in my wildest dreams had I ever contemplated putting my livelihood blessings on paper, or publishing a book.

A good few years back – possibly 1990s – a very good friend of mine, Ingrid, who resides in Durban, South Africa, once said, 'Yvonne, one day I shall write a book on your life story.' But somehow, I have beaten her to it. *Bits And Pieces Of Evita's True Life Story* has already been published, and now we are in the year 2020, dealing with the Covid-19 pandemic which has been causing panic and grief around the world for over a year.

For so many months, we have read that:

Anyone with symptoms, such as a high temperature, continuous cough, or a loss of sense of smell or taste, should isolate.

Vaccines were being produced and tested.

Trace, tracking, and testing was introduced.

And personal protective equipment (PPE) has to be worn for personal protection in hospitals, all over the world.

Since March 2019, we have seen lockdowns around the world to keep people safe, the elderly isolating, advice to keep one's distance from one another, no different households to mix, and the wearing of masks. All these measures are designed to save our National Health Service (NHS) and one another. Added to that, people with underlying health conditions have been advised to shield themselves, while the rest of us follow the rules on keeping our distance, staying at home, wearing masks, washing our hands, and avoiding contact with others.

We all clapped our sanitised hands, and thanked our NHS for their devoted assistance to all the people having suffered from the Covid-19. Unfortunately, many lives have been lost, and many blessings and prayers are needed for all our families worldwide. May they Rest In Peace.

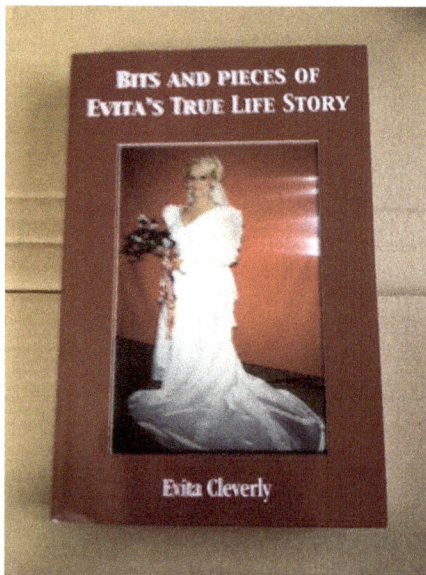

After 39 years, my book *Bits And Pieces Of Evita's True Life Story* was finally published in July 2020, during the Covid-19 Pandemic. Praise Our Heavenly Father.

And it just seems so unreal that all those years have subsided, and somehow I now find myself putting pen to paper again.

I shall now introduce you to my most interesting inspirations, also going back many years, having composed and written lyrics.

My Prayers and Poems in song. May the Lord bless and keep you, through all the years!

JESUS, I THANK THEE.

Jesus, I thank thee, Jesus I thank thee.
I shall always praise thy Holy name,
You will always be in my heart.
Jesus, I thank thee. Jesus, I thank thee.
Jesus, I thank thee from the bottom of my heart.
We have so much to thank Him for.
We have our lives to thank Him for,
We have one another to thank Him for.
Jesus, I thank thee. Jesus, I thank thee,
For the flowers that grow, the trees,
Green grass, and the snow.
Jesus, I thank thee. Jesus, I thank thee,
For all the wonders around,
As I wonder and go wandering.
Jesus, I thank thee. Jesus, I thank thee.

*Written and composed in song and prayer by Yvonne Woods, 1981*

I dedicate this book, *Evita's True Life Story - Since I Was Saved* To my four wonderful children – Floyd, my one and only son (Sonshine); my late daughter Rene (Petal), may she rest in peace; Amalene, my eldest daughter (Girl); and Shiralee, my youngest daughter, (Girlie).

And also to my god-daughter Adele, and late godmother Aunt Kay

I was born Yvonne, in Salisbury (Harare), Rhodesia (Zimbabwe) in 1941, with fair hair and eyes of blue. I eventually grew to a height of 5ft. 2ins, which sounds like a popular song of days gone by: '5ft. 2, eyes of blue'!

*Me as a baby, walking at nine months of age, with a budgerigar on my shoulder*

I commenced my first years of education at a small school named Nettleton Junior School in Salisbury, when I was just five years old.

*My late parents, Thomas and Elizabeth, in 1940.*
*May they Rest in Peace.*

By the time I reached the age of about ten years, our family – Mum, Dad, two sisters, Shirley and Jeannette, and my one and only brother Tyrone, left Salisbury to reside in a beautiful little town in Rhodesia named Umtali (Mutare).

*My brother Tyrone, his wife Tersia, our sisters Jeannette and Shirley, not forgetting the furry family, Jessie and Patches, are pictured in 2020, before the pandemic lockdowns in South Africa*

*My youngest sister Jeannette, sister Shirley,*
*brother Tyrone, and yours truly, pictured together in*
*South Africa in 2016*

I then attended Umtali Junior School, where I tried to progress as a student. I loved my schooling and usually made the top seven in class. Although I was not a very bright spark, I always made the grade. Athletics, however, played a very big part in my life.

My Prayer and Poem also in Song: I AM HAPPY NOW

I am happy now,
You are the first in my life,
I know beauty and peace, and myself.
Where I work, what I do,
Are exchangeable values,
You are not, you are not.
There's not much more to life.
I'd be happy to find,
You by my side,
With beauty and peace.
Where I live, what I do,
Are exchangeable values,
You are not, you are not.

*Composed and written by Yvonne Woods, 1982*

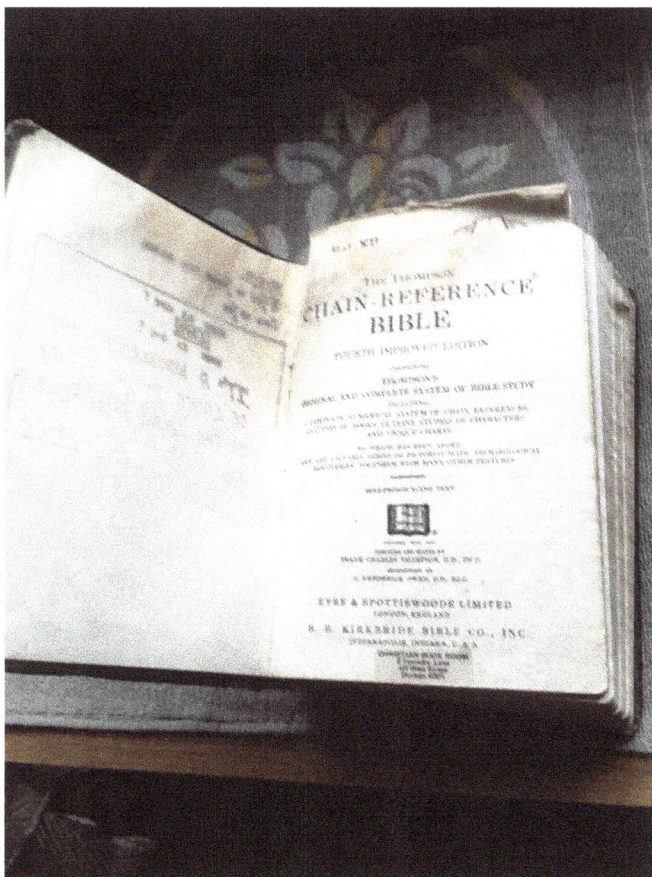

*My first Bible, gifted to me by Rufus, a business client of the company I was employed with. A dream come true.*

Sundays involved the usual Church service, which one was made to attend. Although I remember receiving a prize for progress in Religious Knowledge, I still found I never really understood religion. I never prayed and I never really believed but, having said that, I was always afraid that God could see me.

9

As far as I was concerned, religion was too much like history, which was my weakest and most detested subject, with geography being the next disliked subject. And of course, learning about Jesus, His birth and places He had visited, all centred on geography and history.

I absorbed very little religious knowledge, except that I always remembered Jesus's place of birth, Bethlehem. My knowledge of the greatest man, though, was very little.

As the years go by, we get older and I think we learn by our mistakes, but it is now that I know there is only one way we learn. I shall explain later as the chapters go on.

As years went by, I was a teenager at the Umtali (Matare) Girls High School, Rhodesia (Zimbabwe). School days there were tremendous, and there was never a day I could remember that was not enjoyable.

My school uniform was a very smart dress that I wore with great pride, in green and gold, with a white shirt and green and gold tie. Part of our daily learning, at school, was of Jesus. In Religious Education/Scripture Union, I never managed to win any more prizes, as nothing just ever sunk into my brain. It was beyond me. I believed we are just born, everything is just here, and we take it as it comes.

By the time I had reached almost seventeen years, tragedy struck. I lost my father, Thomas – the man I dearly loved, and no-one could take his place. I could not understand how the Lord works and why this should happen.

I left school without graduating, due to circumstances, and became a hard-working little lady with a splendid company, where my late father had worked. The company director, a lovely Greek gentleman, Deon, had always said that when I left school, he would like me to be his private and confidential secretary. Unbelievably, I was soon in that role!

This company was kind enough to give me the opportunity to attend Secretarial College classes in the afternoons, so I worked by mornings and learnt by afternoons, eventually becoming a Stenographer.

Unfortunately, that wasn't long-lived, as the company had to close its doors. However, all was not lost as they found me another job, as company secretary to a panel beating firm owned by Roy. What a Godsend! I often wonder and think of how many people were as blessed as I was.

My career ended, though, when I fell in love. When you are so young, love seems like everything and we think we know all about it.


I married John, whom I had met through the panel beating company I was employed with. He had met with an accident, so his car ended up at the same panel beater's company. I then became a mother and a farmer's wife, which was wonderful.

*My good-looking son Floyd (Sonshine), whom I saw many years later, had a tattoo on his chest of his late sister, my daughter Rene (Pearl), who was lost out at sea in New Zealand. May she Rest in Peace!*

And by the time I reached the age of 21 years, I had given birth to my first two wonderful children – a handsome son Floyd (Sonshine), and a beautiful daughter Rene (Pearl).

*My beautiful late daughter, Rene (Pearl),*
*lost out at sea. October 21$^{st}$, 1979.*

As the years went by, I attended Church services when I could, but living way out of the little town in the farming community meant it was not always easy to attend. I have already mentioned that I did not understand the Lord right up to my adulthood, and there was so much going on with two children to take care of, along with a home and the staff, that I never had much time for Jesus.

As the years passed by, for some unknown reason things in my home were not going well and eventually that dreaded word 'divorce' took place. The unhappiness is just not easy to explain'; it must be experienced to really understand. Now I had not only lost my father, but my family, too. I thought the tears would never subside!

At this stage of my life, I was almost 29 years old, and was faced with starting my working life again, because I had been a housewife for some time. I began again, in credit control, at a huge department store, which was very enjoyable. But I no longer lived in a beautiful home with all the comforts of housegirls, chefs, and the laughter of my children. Instead, I was living in a pokey residential hotel room, which I shared with another girl to save money.

My second marriage – to Peter. (Strangely enough, my very first boyfriend was called Peter.)

Shortly after I started earning a salary, I met my second husband-to-be, Peter, who was an atheist. We were married in court, as no church would marry us. This was another terrible upset in my life, and something I never understood. I'd always tried to do the correct things like being married in church, as is said 'Build your love on a strong foundation'.

My two younger children, daughters Amalene and Shiralee, were born three years into my second marriage. They were extremely beautiful girls, and still are. After the unhappiness of losing my previous family, I was now slowly smothered by the happiness of my new one, and the two girls – being so close in age – kept me on my toes. There was still no time for Jesus, especially in my husband's eyes, so no christenings for the girls. That is something else that hurt me for many years.

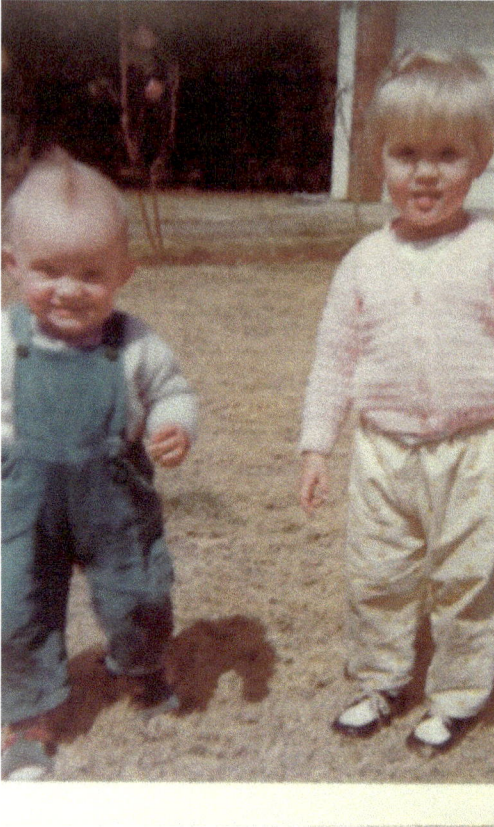

*My youngest daughter, Shiralee, and
eldest daughter, Amalene*

Everything appeared to be blooming, when tragedy hit the family again, and my stepfather, Robert, died. It was heartbreaking, and the pain of all the other memories came flooding back. It was as though we were just getting up the hill and everything going well when suddenly, 'Boom' – something would go wrong and down we would come.

*Me in 2016*

As someone who found it difficult to believe, I ranted and raved when my children would say they had learned at school that God made them. I would scream at them and say, 'I made you; I had you in my tummy; I made your arms and your legs.' But then I'd stop and think about my mother, and her mother. Where did all these mothers come from? 'Well,' my husband Peter said, 'from the pre-historic days.' But I still could not understand where they had originated from, and found myself becoming very exhausted, frustrated and very confused.

In 1981, by which time I'd reached that good old age of being fat and 40, that is when it all happened. I was saved and became a born again Christian. I became a new child of God in May 1981, and I shall remember that year and the month of May as my birthday forever.

My Prayer and Poem, also in song.
IT'S A BEAUTIFUL DAY

It's a beautiful day
It's a beautiful day.
Have you ever thought
Of the lovely day to pray?
It's a beautiful day,
It's a beautiful day.
The skies are so clear,
Good things are near.
It's a lovely day,
It's a lovely day.
We praise thy name, Lord,
We praise thy name.
It's a lovely day,
It's a beautiful day.
It's a beautiful day,
It's a lovely day,
So, let us pray now,
And tell Him, we love Him so,
That we long to be with Him
For as long, as long, as long.
Have you ever thought
Of the lovely day to pray?
It's a lovely day,
It's a beautiful day.
It's a lovely day,
It's a beautiful day.

*Composed and written by Yvonne Woods, 1982*

My Prayer And Poem, also in song
BOP, BOP, BOP FOR THE LORD.

Bop, bop, bop for the Lord,
He will be pleased.
Bob, bop, bop for the Lord,
And sing His holy name.
Jesus, Jesus, is the Lord.
Jesus is Lord.
Bop, bop, bop for the Lord,
Praise His holy name.
Bop, bop, bop for the Lord,
And sing Hallelujah.
Jesus Hallelujah,
Jesus is the Lord,

*Written and Composed By Yvonne Woods, 1984*

My Prayer and Poem, also in song
THE ONLY WAY

Which way, any way, up here, down there?
Oh Lord, is good enough for me.
The only way is to the Lord.
Anyway, whatever way, fast or slow,
Oh Lord, is good enough for me.
The only way is to the Lord,
Car rides, plane rides, or merry-go-rounds,
Oh Lord, is good enough for me.
The only way is to the Lord.

*Written and composed by Yvonne Woods, 1981*

I must explain what eventually led me to the Lord. As I have already explained, I was a switchboard operator and I would speak to hundreds and thousands of people every day, working with one of the biggest estate agencies in Kwa Zulu Natal, Durban, South Africa. Although these people were just voices, they were like friends that we never meet. It was always lovely to speak to them, but on one particular day, this deep, manly, strong voice came over my earpiece and started to compliment me on my telephone manner.

He said I was worth a million, and that he was a big businessman from Pretoria, South Africa, and if I was interested in a job at twice my current rate of pay, to please telephone him at a certain hotel where he was staying in Durban, and we could possibly discuss it over dinner one night.

It all sounded super, except that I was extremely happy in the job I was doing. I had wonderful bosses and colleagues, so I was not at all interested in contacting this businessman about the position offered. I must admit, for the first time in my life, this was one voice that I would have so loved to have put a face to, but under no circumstances was I going to telephone him.

Well, the days went by and then, wow, this voice was back on the line and I put him through to the necessary party. Unbeknown to me, the gentleman was in the middle of a few big business transactions with our company. At the end of the day, the switchboard rang and I answered. It was one of the managers on the line, wanting to know what time I would be finishing up that evening.

When I explained that it was my late night and I would be working until 4.45pm, he asked me to pop into his office on my way down as he had someone who wanted to meet me.

I had to go past his office on my way out of the building, but when I got there, I found this 6ft. 4ins tall, good-looking gentleman, named Rufus. He was just the type of man most girls dream of meeting until you realise – as I do now – that it is not the outside that counts but the inside and what comes from the heart. This gentleman was the one with the deep, strong, manly voice I had heard so many times before, and I was really taken aback.

He invited me to dinner and we spent a most beautiful evening, during which he praised the Lord, speaking only of Him in tongues. I was at an absolute loss as I did not understand this foreign language and, least of all, why he should praise the Lord the way he did. The only thing that came to my mind was that this big, burly man was an absolute maniac, just heading for the lunatic asylum and was not for me.

It was actually the second time in my life I'd heard the Lord's name being praised.

Shortly before meeting Rufus, I was taken to visit a lady in hospital called Rea. She was a friend of my friend, Lawrence, and they both praised Jesus's loving name. I just sat beside her, not understanding but truly thinking that she must have had a bad accident in which she'd knocked her head very badly and was losing her mind. This ran through my mind the whole of the visiting hour, during which time I never said a word. As I had never said or mentioned the Lord's name in many a year, I was surely not about to start now!

When Rufus took me home after our dinner, he said, 'Yvonne, I would like you to do something for me.

I think you are a wonderful person and I, being a child of God, couldn't even contemplate marrying you,' He wasn't making a promise, just giving an explanation me to, Christian to non–Christian, 'unless you became a child of God. Wouldn't you please attend a church service? I cannot take you, as it is something you must do on your own accord and not because you just want to see what it is all about, but because you really feel you want to attend.'

I agreed that I would do that, but whether or not I was actually going to go was another matter.

The following Sunday evening arrived, and I knew the church service was at 7pm, but I certainly had no intention of attending.

(a)  It was dark.
(b)  I had no transport.
(c)  What a waste of money for a taxi.

Excuse after excuse, ran through my head, then my telephone rang at 6.50pm. It was Rufus.

'Yvonne, are you going to the service at 7pm?'

I immediately offered an excuse. 'I cannot, I do not have any transport.'

He said, 'Couldn't you catch a taxi?'

'I do not have any money.'

Rufus replied, 'I shall send someone to collect you.'

I still argued, 'No! No! I shall see if a friend of mine can take me.'

'OK,' said Rufus. And we said good night.

By this time, it was 6.55pm, and all I was concerned about was delaying this whole episode. I was truly hoping when I phoned this friend of mine, Lawrence, that there would be no reply so I wouldn't have to ask a favour; it just was not done.

I held on to the receiver as the call rang, then suddenly he answered. Now I am hoping before popping the question that he will be otherwise occupied and unable to take me.

'Lawrence, I would like to ask you a very big favour,' I started. It was now 7pm. *Hooray*! I thought. "Please could you give me a lift to the church service?'

If I had been any closer than a phone call away, I'm sure he would have kissed me with excitement. Lawrence was so pleased and that was when I learned he was a re-born Christian. I had suspected it, but Lawrence respected my views and had never really pushed me as far as the Lord was concerned.

Suddenly, the rush was on. The church service had already commenced and we would be late, but my friend nevertheless dashed over to collect me on his motorcycle. I was petrified of the motorcycle, as my father had met his death on one of those machines.

He arrived within minutes and off we went to the service. By the time we arrived, it was well underway so we chose a seat in the back row. I did not want to get too close or too involved, because it had been a long time since I had said a prayer and I was afraid people would see I didn't know how to pray.

We sat, I listened, I watched…and then it happened! The Pastor was calling for all those who didn't believe, or thought they might, or who would like to, to rise and come forward. I was determined that under no circumstances was I going to join them, and sat even more rigid, desperate not to move.

I do not know what happened or how it happened, but people had stopped standing up to join the Pastor when suddenly, I was up on my feet, I could no longer sit. I just had to go! So down the aisle I went with tears streaming down my cheeks!

Then things started happening. I was so afraid. I felt completely on my own, yet there were many people around me. I felt like a school child about to be questioned and would not know the answers.

Eight months previously, I had met a girl called Carol, whom I had immediately liked. But with her being a Christian and me a non-believer, nothing had ever come of our friendship. Even after I had given her my name and telephone number and asked her to please give me a call, time went on and there was no word from her. At the time, I felt quite hurt.

But now, as I was standing in this church waiting to meet the Pastor, this voice spoke to me. 'Hello, Yvonne.' And when I looked up, there was Carol! I was so overwhelmed, I couldn't even remember her name.

By this stage in the proceedings, the Pastor had spoken to many people. When he touched them lightly on the top of their heads, I watched as they just fell to the ground. I felt so nervous. I had never believed in hypnosis or been a superstitious person, and I just did not know what was happening.

Then it was my turn, and I found myself lying on the floor. I don't know if I slept or what, but I was weeping as I awoke, crying louder than when my father died and when I lost my late daughter. I was completely drained and my mind was so empty I felt light-headed.

I was helped into a sitting position and asked to put my name and telephone number on a card I had been handed. But when the lady who was assisting me looked at my card, she said, 'That is not your name.' I felt so nervous, and was wondering if I had stumbled into some voodoo or witchcraft and was losing my mind. I looked at my card and assured her, 'That is my name. I know my name!'

She looked surprised and told me, 'But that is *my* name. Yvonne Woods.'

I was absolutely shocked, because I had known about this Yvonne Woods for almost four years.

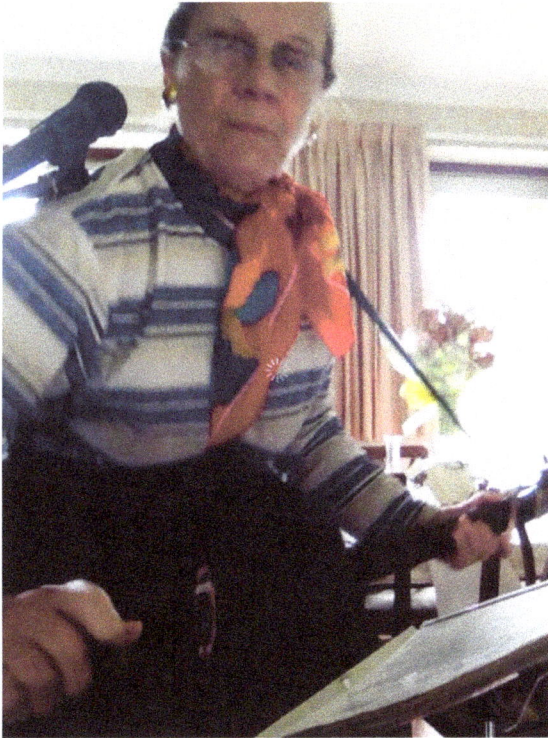

*I sang in ladies bars for my family's bread and butter, as we had migrated from Rhodesia (Zimbabwe)*

How that came about was that I used to sing in the ladies' bars to earn a bit of money when we needed it. This was when I was married, and a couple of years after we arrived in Kwa Zulu Natal, Durban. On occasions, I would receive a telephone call at the company where I was employed, but the caller had the wrong Yvonne, as they were asking me to take part in the church service. It seems the Yvonne I had not met yet did a great deal for the Lord.

It became a huge joke to think that I was going to sing for the Lord. 'Oh, no,' I would say, 'I only sing for the alkies and boozers.' The caller would be amazed they had the wrong Yvonne. She apparently had fair hair, eyes of blue, was a little taller than me and a little younger, too. And she was a beautiful person.

So that moment when we both met was when I finally knew that there is a Lord. He brought us, two Yvonne Woods, together. Not another solitary soul could ever have done that, as there was no-one who knew even my name whilst I was at that Church service. How I praised the Lord! And I shall never stop praising His loving name, as that was one of His miracles.

That was just the beginning of my life as a Christian. I have so much more to yell and shout about, I am so happy. Whilst this was going on, Rufus was wanting to know what was taking place, and he was overjoyed when he heard.

I was still feeling very drained the next day, and I almost had to refresh my mind with my telephone numbers and so on.

My Prayer and Poem, also in song
I AM HAPPY NOW

I am happy now,
You are the first in my life,
I know beauty and peace,
And myself.
Where I work, what I do,
Are exchangeable values,
You are not.
There's not much more to life,
I'd be happy to find,
You by my side,
With beauty and peace.
Where I live, what I do,
Are exchangeable values,
You are not. You are not.

I do hope that you are happy now.

*Composed and written by Yvonne Woods, 1981*

Another couple of days went by and my children were coming to see me. Rufus was looking forward to meeting them, and he arrived with gifts, including a beautiful Bible for the children. 'It is a gift from Jesus,' he told them.

This was very new to them, but they loved it.

Then out came the other gift from Jesus. 'For Mum,' explained Rufus.

It was beautiful, a pair of praying hands in a frame, inscribed with 'Bless This House'. But what Rufus, and not even my closest family, ever knew was how I had longed my whole life to own a pair of beautiful praying hands.

You see, I did not dare mention Jesus's name in those days of being a non-believer, for fear that people thought

I was insane, but obviously, deep, deep down, I had a spark of Jesus in me! Even I never knew that I would ever see this lovely day where I would praise His loving name to all. There we are, some more works of the Lord. Isn't it wonderful?

By this stage of my life, the rosiness around me was unreal and the people I spoke to through my job were so complimentary. Of course, I had received many a compliment over the years due to my telephone manner throughout the whole day! It was so exciting, and I just could not control this bubbling all over, bursting at the seams feeling. What a tonic! As a result, I was even meeting Christians on the other end of the telephone line, and we would praise the Lord.

I'd like to point out that I am not a Bible thumper, religious maniac or freak. I am simply stating true facts and experiences I have had in real life, my life; not in a dream.

*I was beginning to understand and appreciate*
*Jesus in my heart*

My Prayer and Poem, in song
I WANT TO SING FOR YOU, DEAR LORD

I want to sing for you, dear Lord,
I want to sing for you, dear Lord.
So, let us begin to sing for Him a song.
We will praise Him,
We will love Him,
We will thank Him, till the end.
Those will be my words to you, dear Lord.
Those will be my words to you dear Lord.
We will ask for forgiveness,
We will ask for love,
We will ask for rest,
Till the end.
Those will be my words to you, dear Lord,
Those will be my words to you, dear Lord.
From this day on,
I want to sing for you, dear Lord,
I want to sing for you, dear Lord.
I want to sing, to sing for you, dear Lord.
So, let us begin.
So, let us begin.
The most beautiful thing is to sing.

*Written and composed by Yvonne Woods, 1982*

The days were flying by faster than I have ever known;
the hours were never enough for me in a day. I found
I could get to bed late in the evenings, but I was
also being woken early in the mornings. I couldn't
understand this until I read that the first break of dawn
is where we get our strength through the Lord.

Eventually, I would say my prayers last thing, and when I awakened at that early hour of 3am, I would thank Jesus again for the lovely day to come and all I was about to receive, then I would fall off to sleep.

Somehow, though I always woke on time to get ready for work and was never late. I was so blessed that I no longer used my wrist watch or alarm clock. Yet when I turned my bedside radio on in the mornings, the announcer would tell the hour and I'd find I was never woken later than usual. I used my radio just to check the hour, as I was not yet accustomed to the Lord's assistance and was still testing Him. I found myself testing Him on many occasions.

All this happened to me, really, within a week. But the next work of the Lord was to come without my knowledge. My ex-flat mate, Margaret, rang me one Sunday evening asking if I would like to join her at her new flat, as she was having a small get-together. She wanted me to come along so that I could see her new flat, as I had previously missed the flat-warming party. I accepted but explained that I would first be attending the church service, which only finished at around 9.45pm.

It was agreed that Margaret would collect me outside the service at 9pm, as I thought the Lord would excuse me. But when I was sitting in the church, I became a little concerned that I had made this appointment and how on earth I was going to be able to stick to 9pm when I no longer wore a wrist watch. Well, after an hour of the service, I couldn't stand it any more and asked the people sitting in front of me if they could please let me know the time. It was 8pm – one whole hour before meeting Margaret. How on earth am I going to make it?

The people sitting ahead of me left shortly after, and I was left sitting with a few empty seats around me. It meant that if I wanted to ask the hour, I would have to get up and go over to someone. I felt a little on the shy side, then told myself: *Stop worrying, you came to enjoy the Church service and that is what you are going to do. Sit back, the Lord will see to it.* As you see, I was testing the Lord again.

We sang, we prayed for the sick, for ourselves, we thanked the Lord, and the next thing I knew the service was over and I was still sitting there. I had enjoyed myself so very much that I had forgotten what I was supposed to do. At that stage, it was too late to worry if I didn't make it on time, so I proceeded to go out with all the congregation.

As I got outside on the pavement, I could see no sign of my ex-flatmate, who was very unreliable but I loved her all the same and just accepted her for what she was. Again, I turned around to people just coming out the service to enquire about the hour, and a lady said, '9pm.'

I could not believe it was that hour, but she had no sooner finished answering my question when I felt a tap on my shoulder. I turned to find a complete stranger, a man, touching my shoulder.

'Excuse me,' he said. 'Are you Yvonne?'

'Yes,' I replied, "that's me.'

'Margaret asked me to fetch you.'

Well, I was absolutely amazed how he even knew it was me.

We walked to my friend's flat, my Bible under my arm, and I discussed the whole way there how good the Lord was to me. He was trying to put all sorts of obstacles in my way, but I carried on, hardly even hearing him.

Arrived at Margaret's flat, I got the impression I was to partner someone, and thought, *No way!* I had my usual favourite drink – lovely fresh milk. People are always laughing at me, but I became so intoxicated on the Lord's Spirit, that truly three glasses of milk and I'm finished.

I had a lovely time but decided, after an hour, that it was time I left for home. I thanked Margaret for a lovely evening, remarked on her lovely flat, lifted my Bible, and said good night to everyone. I could not believe what I was doing, getting ready to escort myself home at 10pm, and not wanting a man to escort me back to my flat. The others were a little concerned and asked if I would be alright, but I said I would be and left.

My eyes were as big as saucers by the time the lift arrived. I could not believe that I was on my way home, walking down the street alone at this late hour; I had never in my whole life been so brave. I even slept with a light burning through the night.

But as the lift landed on the ground floor and the doors opened, I said, 'Oh well, Jesus, this is where you take over now. I am in your hands.'

I had no sooner turned the corner into the Victoria Embankment street, when I heard a noise behind me. I thought, *This is it. Again, Lord, you have let me down. This is the end of my life. I am about to be attacked and robbed.*

But as I looked back over my shoulder, I couldn't believe it. There, behind me, was a policeman, and he walked all the way behind me and got into the same lift at my block of flats. I pressed the lift button number eleven, and he pressed number twelve, then he looked at the Bible under my arm and asked what I was studying.

I explained that I had just been to a church service and this was my Bible I was still studying. I didn't realise it then, but I know now, that there is so much to learn from the good book; if only we realised this as youngsters.

The lift stopped, I said, 'Good night,' and off I went to my flat.

Now, there is no way one could ring the police and ask to be escorted home. So how did that happen? The Lord is the greatest.

A Prayer and Poem I have read so many times
WHEN I SING FOR HIM

When I sing for Him, oh, praise God's holy name,
I can feel His presence in my soul.
When I sing for Him, oh, blessed be His name.
How I rejoice within when I sing for Him.
As I sing a melody, that He gave,
When I speak God's name in song,
Or kneel to pray,
Oh, I have a special feeling deep within.
When I sing for Him.
When I sing for Him.
Hallelujah! When I move to my new home.
Hallelujah! Oh, the angels will be singing.
Hallelujah! Amen.

*Unknown composer*

*I was escorted to my home by an unknown policeman,*
*in Kwa Zulu-Natal, South Africa. The Lord truly works*
*in mysterious ways.*

Family and friends, don't think it all ends there. There
are a lot more of the Lord's good works that I can tell
you about – true experiences that have happened to me.

It was always my longing to own a beautiful replica of *The Lord's Last Supper And The Twelve Disciples* painting by Leonardo da Vinci. I was house-sitting for my young daughter Shiralee's family, who were migrating to New Zealand, and their home was up for sale. I moved to the flatlet on the property, only to find that a replica of *The Lord's Last Supper And The Twelve Disciples* had been left hanging on the wall. No-one had claimed it! I couldn't believe it.

Anyway, after the property was sold, I found myself investing in a new venture – a holiday home where I lived but let out to holidaying families when I was away. And what did I find hanging above the bed in the main bedroom? A beautiful, home-made wall plaque, which featured The Lord's Last Supper And The Twelve Disciples! I was absolutely taken aback, but it was another answered prayer. May I just say, not a solitary soul, family or friends, had ever known of my desire to own this painting.

*My replica painting by Leonardo da Vinci,* The Lord's Last Supper And The Twelve Disciples

By the way, the Bible which was gifted to me by Rufus, was the first in my whole life. It was something again I had always wanted, but was waiting and praying to receive as a gift.

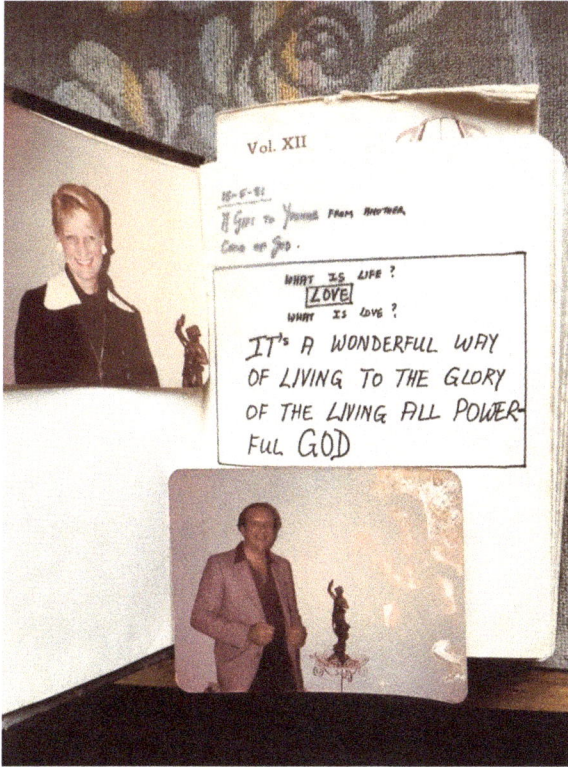

*My first Bible, gifted to me by Rufus –*
*one of my dreams come true!*

The month of May was a beautiful month that year (1981). And by the middle of June, so much had been done for me – this young child of God – through Jesus, in such a short period of time. Not long after applying,

I became a South African citizen, and was very excited to know this was now my home.

That month, I met a new friend, Hadrian. He was 6ft. with soft, dreamy eyes, and we started seeing quite a bit of one another. One day, during my lunch hour, I laid my head down for a brief rest and had the strangest dream. It was Thursday afternoon, 25th June, and I could see fresh, bright red blood pouring from below me; the cleanest, reddest, freshest blood I have ever seen.

On awakening, I mentioned my strange dream to my colleague, Anne, who sat at the switchboard next to mine. However, I thought no more of it and when the day ended, I dashed back to my flat, as I had a very special dinner date that evening.

The hours fly when one is bathing and shampooing and so on, and in the midst of my preparations, my mother telephone me and we chatted for a while. I didn't dare tell her I would be going out on a motorcycle, as she would have worried herself sick.

After that telephone conversation, the phone rang again. This time, it was Rufus, the gentleman who introduced me to the Lord. He said he needed to have a bit of fellowship and wanted particularly to speak with a certain pastor in Durban, so he would be coming to the city shortly. I had never heard of the pastor he referred to, but thought it would be lovely to see Rufus again.

*Ready for my motorcycle date with Hadrian*

At long last I was ready awaiting my date, Hadrian, and he arrived at the scheduled time. We took off on our evening out, riding on his beautiful motorcycle, which was black chrome and gold trimmed. We had a lovely Chinese supper, but I was worrying and brooding over what my good man's intentions might be after the evening was over. It was terribly wrong of me to have had such wild thoughts, but unfortunately, we do on occasions meet with mishaps. So, I was contemplating the whole time as to how I was going to avoid the inevitable.

The Lord, however, took care of that, as I just didn't get back to my flat. Instead, we met with such a freak accident.

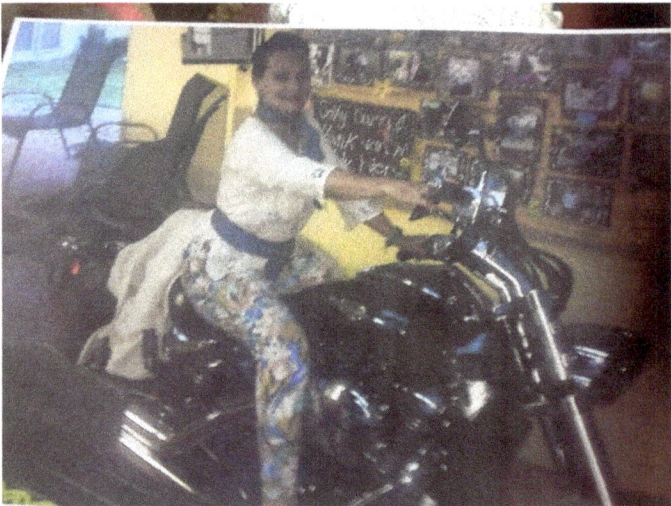

*Me on the motorcycle*

I could not believe this was happening to me. It was like a slow-motion movie, with the glass breaking in the background and me landing on the ground. I was grabbing at my damaged leg, which was almost off at the knee, but I did not have enough hands to hold my squashed leg. I heard myself suddenly yelling, then suddenly I stopped and asked myself why I was shouting when I knew that God would look after me.

From that moment on, I was beaming and smiling, my eyes bluer and shinier than ever, and I felt like a teenager again. I cannot ever explain this experience, which I once again received from the Lord.

Whilst all this was taking place, I never enquired about Hadrian; it was as though I knew he was fine. I had given everyone my name, telephone number, address, where to contact my parents, my age, where I was employed, my friend's name and address.

There were quite a number of people around, but no-one appeared to know what to do until suddenly a gentleman appeared. Robin was a Rhodesian/ Zimbabwean Army Medic on holiday in Durban, South Africa. He was a very big Christian, speaking in religious tongues, which was unbelievable but I had to believe it as it was happening before my very eyes.

I heard him explain that he was on his way to take the babysitter to her home but lost his way back to where he was staying and ended up at my accident. He referred to verses from the Bible, prayed, then took his jacket off to keep me warm. He then removed his tie and applied it to my thigh as a tourniquet.

Robin, my brother through Christ, saved my life, with the guidance of the Lord. The calmness, the quietness, the smoothness of every move he made just step by step, and absolutely nothing went wrong. His prayers were answered.

In the interim, a young university student, Stephen, who was studying to be a doctor, was jogging by and came across my accident. He insisted on accompanying me in the ambulance, and took off the t-shirt he was wearing and had a bystander dampen it so that he could use it to wet my very dry lips.

The Police arrived, then the ambulance, and before we knew it we were at Addington Hospital in Durban. The one thing I will praise and thank the Lord for is the painlessness of it all. I had no pain from the beginning of the accident right up to the x-rays being taken and my clothes being cut/stripped off me. Oh, I will never stop praising His loving name for that.

I was taken into the theatre where they operated from 1am until 4am on Friday, 26th June, 1981 and what a lovely Friday. My toes, I could move; my leg had been stitched back on below the knee; a steel pin had been inserted in the one big bone of my leg (tibia); and the little bone (fibula) had two breaks. A big part of bone was missing and there was a huge, gaping wound, so my leg was in quite a mess. But this is where the Lord acted again. The orthopaedic specialist was given the inspiration to see how he could save my leg through answered prayer. Only answered prayer could have done it.

My mother and David, my second stepfather, had been contacted and by this stage had been informed of possible amputation. I had also heard the medical staff say amputation, but I was given such strength and courage that it did not at any time bother me. The feeling of contentment had set in, and I knew it would never happen.

I cannot explain the peace that I received. 'Thank you, Jesus,' was all I could say, even though it seemed such a feeble little thank you for all that he was doing for me.

My Prayer and Poem, also in song
JESUS, I THANK THEE

Jesus, I thank thee.
Jesus, I thank thee,
I shall always praise thy name,
You will always be in my heart.
Jesus, I thank thee, Jesus, I thank thee,
Jesus, I thank thee,
From the bottom of my heart.

We have so much to thank Him for,
We have one another, to thank Him for.
Jesus, I thank thee, Jesus, I thank thee,
For the flowers that grow, the trees,
Green grass, and the snow.

Jesus, I thank thee, Jesus, I thank thee.
Jesus, I thank thee,
For all the wonders around me,
As I wonder and go wandering.
Jesus, I thank thee, Jesus, I thank thee.
Jesus, I thank thee.
I shall always praise thy name,
You will always be in my heart.
Jesus, I thank thee,
Jesus, I thank thee,
From the bottom of my heart.

*Written and composed by Yvonne Woods, 1981*

It was only on awakening after the operation that I saw
Hadrian, in a wheelchair, not looking himself and in
terrible pain. He had apparently suffered a hip out of
joint, a grazed right leg, and swelling in the knee and
ankle. Praise the Lord, it was not too serious. I could

never have accepted the thought of my friend lying badly injured in the other end of the hospital, and I in the opposite side, unable to see one another.

He was soon on his feet with a walking stick, and a day later he was discharged from the hospital. But every single day as I lay there, he was at my bedside; not a day did he miss. Oh, how I thank Jesus for such a wonderful friend.

He felt my every moment, and there *were* moments of pain. After all, I am human, and made of flesh and blood. But the pain was at odd intervals and for only split moments. Considering what I had undergone, it was unbelievable that I could be so comfortable and pain-free, a. Another work of the Lord.

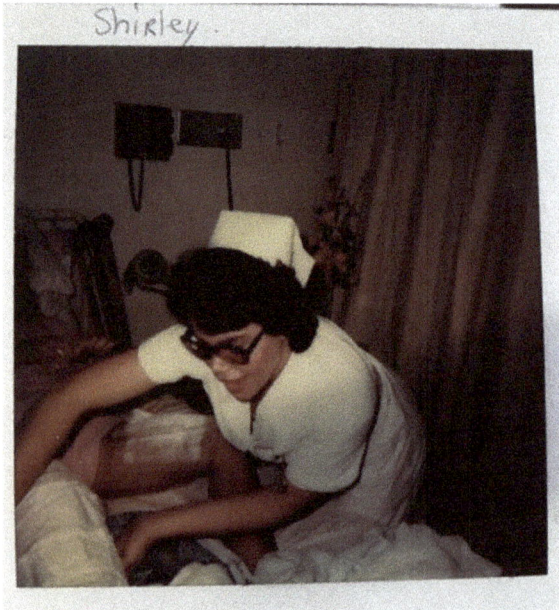

*My nurse, Shirley, in Addington Hospital, Durban*

My nurses were tremendous and I say many prayers for them, but I need to say what a blessing it was to have one of them sharing the same name as my sister, Shirley. Nurse Shirley was beside me in Addington Hospital, Durban, and along with many other nurses, attended to my wounds, comfort, and many needs. Together in the morning and evening we sang my beautiful prayers, which were composed and written in the ward of Addington Hospital, and this link was another wonder which God sent into my life at that time.

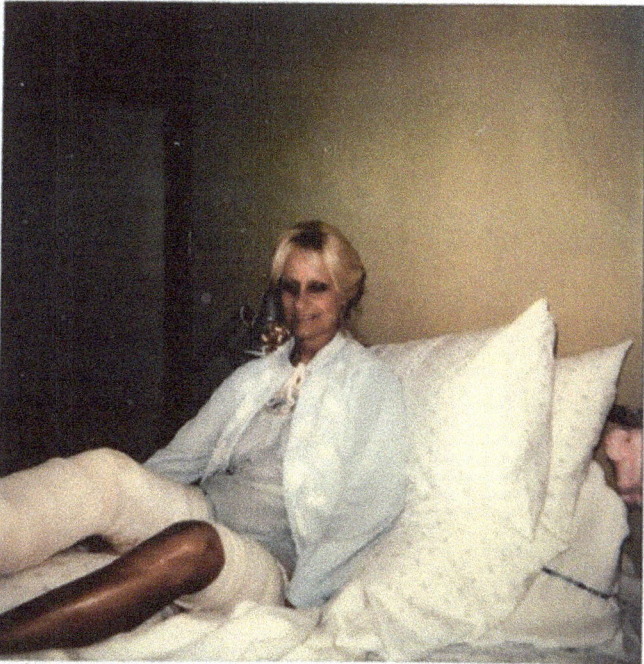

*After my motorcycle accident, awaiting the verdict on whether my leg would need to be amputated. I had the company of my little pink elephant, which was a gift from my daughters, Amalene and Shiralee. Praise The Lord.*

My Prayer and Poem, also in song
JESUS TAKE MY HEART

Take my heart, Jesus.
Jesus, take my heart.
Take my heart, Jesus,
Never be apart.
I will always love you,
Till the day I die.
Take my heart,
Jesus, take my heart,
And never let it part.
You need the world,
The world needs you, too.
Jesus, my world,
Is all my world in you.
Take my heart, Jesus.
Jesus, take my heart.
Take my heart, Jesus,
And never be apart.
Jesus, I need you,
All away along the line.
Jesus, please, please be mine.
Take my heart, Jesus.
Jesus, take my heart.
Please, please, be my part,
Jesus, please, please be my part.

*Written and composed by Yvonne Woods, 1981*

As a result of the dirt on the roadside, a little infection
set in the wound, but I still felt on top of the world.
I just kept thanking Jesus. To combat the infection,

the nurses had to inject me with antibiotics, and they would sympathise with me before administering the jab in case it caused me pain. But I never felt the injections.

One nurse asked, 'Didn't that hurt?'

I said, "Nurse, I am not being untruthful, but honestly I didn't feel it.' She just shook her head in disbelief and walked away.

This treatment went on for twenty days, every six hours, as I had to have a double dose. Eventually, it was over. I did feel the last one, but it was nothing to cry over, at all. I thank Jesus for the painlessness.

At this point, I would like to take you back to the first day of the accident – Friday, 26th June, 1981, and you may also remember how the Lord brought my namesake Yvonne and I together. Well, he did it again. Yvonne, my namesake, had to make a telephone call to someone at the company I was employed with, but she did not know I worked there.

As often happens, the person wasn't there, so a message was left. 'Please,' the caller Yvonne said, 'ask them to call me back. My name is Yvonne.'

The operator, my colleague, said, 'But are you our Yvonne?' meaning me.

Yvonne had regular dealings with my company, so she considered herself to be one of us, and replied, 'Yes.'

'But,' said the operator, "did you not have an accident this morning?'

'No,' Yvonne replied.

'You do have blonde hair, eyes of blue?' she was asked.

'Yes,' Yvonne replied. Then suddenly realising it was the other Yvonne they were referring to – me – she enquired where I was.

And she appeared as my first sister through Christ at my hospital bedside, and prayed, 'Please, Lord, we shall not hear of amputation again.'

It was lovely to see her, and I thank the Lord for sending her to me. He is truly the greatest.

For all the time I was in hospital – a few weeks, rather than the expected two or three months – I could not understand how Yvonne, my sister through Christ, had known where to find me. I only found out after leaving hospital and meeting her at a church service! Praise the Lord.

The lady, Rea, that I had visited in hospital and heard praising the Lord, actually turned up at my hospital bedside to visit me this time, and she now heard me praising the Lord. She offered me the crutches she used when discharged from the hospital, after I had met her.

I learned that she was also a widow whose husband had been a non-believer, as was mine. My husband had been murdered – shot and killed – while her husband was electrocuted. Both men sadly died when they were only in their forties. Perhaps we may all have our own conclusions, as I praise Jesus!

*Yvonne, blonde hair and blue eyes. 'Are you our Yvonne?'*

For the whole five weeks I was in hospital, I was blessed with the most beautiful flowers; it was like a little garden around me. Chocolates were plentiful, and in particular, Black Magic. I had not had those chocolates for almost thirteen years, but ended up with four boxes. Sweets were plentiful, as were magazines and gifts, from friends I never knew I had – some I had not seen for two or three years. It was absolute bliss, and I thank Jesus for my friends and my family. I thank Him for my life. Amen.

My Prayer And Poem, also in song
EVER TO LOVE THEE

My joy and my victory,
My Lord and my king,
Ever to love thee,
Ever to sing.
Anthems of glory
And praises to thee.
For ever and ever, I will love thee.
The days are so long,
The nights so short,
Thank you, my Lord,
For all you have taught.
Ever to love thee,
Ever to sing,
Anthems of glory,
And promises to thee,
For ever and ever,
I will love thee.

*Composed and written by Yvonne Woods, 1981*

It does not all end there. I had now been given, through the Lord, a wonderful gift – composing and writing songs for the Lord. Even now, I cannot believe how the words just appear, the music just pours out my mouth, and within ten minutes I have written a beautiful song.

As I was a Country and Western singer, I had tried in the past, on several occasions, to write and compose songs, but always found it extremely difficult.

I composed my first song (not Country and Western) in hospital in the early hours of the morning. It is called

'Jesus Loves You, and it became our morning and evening prayer, which was sung for the patients of my ward.

My Prayer and Poem, also in song
JESUS LOVES YOU

Jesus loves you in the morning,
Jesus loves you through the day
Jesus loves you in the evening
And we love Jesus, just the same.

Thank you, Jesus, for the folks we have.
Thank you, Jesus, for the friends we meet.
Thank you, Jesus, for the knowledge you spread.
So many thank yous,
Thank you, Jesus. Jesus, my friend.

*Composed and written by Yvonne Woods, 1981*

This was my first song, when I realised Jesus does really love you, and I wrote it in the hospital. Patients and visitors were amazed that I was allowed to have my tape recorder and guitar at my bedside, and my spiritual verse hanging above my bed up on the hospital wall.

My guitar was part of me in hospital, and so was my tape recorder. My heart was filled so much with joy that I sang and sang. After singing and strumming my guitar for almost two weeks, there was one dear patient who was due to leave hospital, and I prayed I could compose a new song for her before she went home.

Lo and behold, the night before she left, I had composed another song, which I named 'Dear Lord'

This was another prayer I had answered, and I'd like to share some of the others that have happened in this short period of knowing the Lord.

When my first marriage broke up, I was unemployed and could not afford to look after my eldest two children, my son Floyd and my daughter Rene. So, they lived with their father in New Zealand.

Some years later, after my daughter had since been lost at sea, I desperately wanted to send for my son to visit me. I had not been employed at my job for a long time, but decided that once I became permanent staff in June that year (1981), I would send for my son using the fly now, pay later scheme. Too many years and miles had already come between us and I was desperate to see him again.

However, I went on the permanent staff list in the same month that my horrendous motorcycle accident happened, so my plans went out of the window. I have never felt so upset my whole life. It always seemed as though there was a continuous barrier preventing my son and I getting together.

I prayed, 'Lord, there must be some plan you can think of. Please, dear Lord, you know how I long for my son, and how I have tried to plan. Please, Lord, see what you can do.'

My Prayer and Poem, in song
DEAR LORD

Dear Lord, I pray to you,
Dear Lord, for all in pain.
Dear Lord, I pray to you,

Dear Lord, for all in vain.
Dear Lord, I'm sure you know,
Dear Lord, we need you so.
Dear Lord, I pray to you,
Dear Lord, for all I pray.

*Written and composed by Yvonne Woods, 1981*

This song was written and recorded in hospital, and sung by patients and nurses as daily prayers.

I said my prayer and left it at that. Weeks went by as I waited to be discharged from the hospital. On the day I was due to leave, there was a small mishap which delayed my discharge, so I had to stay in hospital another night.

The next day, everything was in order and I was dressed and ready when my friend Hadrian called to collect me. As we left, the nurse handed me my mail. I could not believe there was a letter from my son, saying, 'Dearest Mom, I am coming to see you in February, and that is a fact. We have been apart and too far from one another for too long, and I am coming.'

The tears poured from my eyes and the happiness once again filled my heart. I was bursting with joy. I owe Jesus so many thanks – that is answered prayer, just out of the blue! *What more*, I thought, *could the Lord do for me, this young child of God, who understands and knows so very little*? When I read my Bible, I try so hard but just do not know or understand all that is the word of God. The verses, what magnificent works, so beautiful.

Those are not the only prayers I have had answered. I have prayed for the immediate family, and they have all been answered; it is too magnificent. Thank you, Jesus, thank you.

I try very hard not to ask the Lord for too much for myself, but I know that nothing is too much for him. I do pray to the Lord for others around me, as I have been given this beautiful feeling of wanting to help others. But I find I cannot do it on my own, that I must have the Lord's assistance. We need to love, believe in the Lord, praise the Lord, thank him constantly, include him in our daily living as a companion, close to our hearts.

My Prayer and Poem, in song
TAKE MY HEART JESUS

Take my heart Jesus, Jesus take my heart.
Take my heart Jesus, never be apart.
I will always love you till the day I die.
Jesus take my heart, take my heart, Jesus,
And never let it part.
You need the world, the world needs you, too.
Jesus my world, is all my world in you.
Take my heart, Jesus, Jesus take my heart.
Jesus take my heart, take my heart, Jesus,
And never be apart.
Jesus, I need you, all the way along the line,
Jesus, please, please, be mine.
Take my heart, Jesus, please be my part.
Take my heart, Jesus. Jesus, please, please be my part.

*Written and composed by Yvonne Woods, 1981*

Things have become so fantastic that when my mind begins to turn to others around me and I am just thinking of their wellbeing, the telephone will ring and they will be calling me to see how I am, even from as far off as Johannesburg, South Africa. The Lord works in his own mysterious way. These are not just coincidences, which some people would claim; it happens often and regularly.

On another occasion when I was in hospital in Durban, South Arica, one Sunday morning, my memory was turning over about a couple of cousins of mine, Noel and Mark, who attended university there. Well, that very evening they both appeared at my bedside at visiting hour. One of the brothers, Noel, I hadn't seen for seven years, but I was thrilled to see them both and overwhelmed. Again, I can only say 'Thank you, thank you, Jesus' for such a wonderful happening.

My cousin Noel, whilst in my thoughts, came to
visit me in hospital in Durban

My cousin Mark, Noel's younger brother,
also visited me in hospital

On one occasion, when I was leaving hospital, one of
the nurses asked me to please pray for her husband.
I find that I am asked to pray more and more for various
families. It is a wonderful experience.

To explain these 'events', I have had to go back
through my memories, but there have been so many
wonderful happenings and they all relate and happen at

different periods in my life. Sometimes, though, there are only days between each 'answered prayer'.

I would like to go back to the telephone conversation with Rufus, when he mentioned that he wanted to fellowship with a certain pastor, whose name I had never heard. Well, would you believe, I met the very same pastor's wife – another sister through Christ – the day after my accident. This lovely lady was situated in the bed next to me.

When she was discharged, she presented me with a religious poster which included the words of a certain testimony: 'You ask me how I know He lives, He lives within my heart'. Such beautiful words. This poster was promptly hung above my bed in the hospital ward.

I also met her husband, the pastor, when he came to visit her. It was so unbelievable. First, I had never heard of these people, and the next I was speaking and praying with them. Praise the Lord. He works in such amazingly wonderful ways.

I have so much to praise the Lord for, and in particular my folk who did so much for me when I was recovering from my motorcycle accident.

My Prayer and Poem, in song
I WANT TO SING FOR YOU, DEAR LORD

I want to sing for you, dear Lord.
I want to sing for you, dear Lord.
So, let us begin to sing for Him,
A song, we will praise Him,
We will love Him, to the end.

Those will be my words
To you, Dear Lord.
We will ask for forgiveness,
We will ask for love, We will ask for rest,
Till the end.
Those will be my words to you, dear Lord,
From this day on.

*Written and composed by Yvonne Woods, 1981*

By February 1982, I was still seeing Hadrian, and would spend weekends yachting with him, as he enjoyed this pastime. All the time, I longed to be with my children, but as I did not have my own transport, it was not always so easy. I was wondering in my mind which day would be suitable for my friend to take me to them, when he offered, out of the blue, to collect my children so that they could spend the day with us on the beach. Another answered prayer.

I had asked another friend, John, to take me to see my baby sister, Jeannette, before I left for Johannesburg to meet my son Floyd, who was arriving from New Zealand. At the time, my thoughts went to my elderly Aunt Florence, my baby sister's mother-in-law, and I wondered if John would object to bringing her for the ride. Then, out of the blue again, John offered my Aunt Florence the ride! I truly thank the Lord and praise Him, and ask Him to bless all my friends and their families.

I had the most fantastic inspiration from the Lord to take my guitar and sing a prayer for a friend of my folks (Fyn).

My Prayer and Poem
INSPIRATIONS

Inspirations from the Lord,
Not just good luck, as we all say,
But inspirations from the Lord.
Inspirations, not coincidences,
As we all like to say.
Oh, inspirations from the Lord,
Is a way of His word.
He has a way of getting through to you and I,
As He passes by.
Inspirations from the Lord,
We have all heard.
Oh Lord, thank you, too,
For these inspirations.
Inspirations, the miracles, the healings,
The need of the Lord.
Inspiration is what it's all called.
Inspirations from the Lord
Is what it's called.

*Written and composed by Yvonne Woods, 1982*

The victory is won by not letting other people hold you back or stop you, so we must keep on blooming. I can feel myself blooming, but praise the Lord if you are not blooming the correct way. He has a way of slowly letting it fade away then, hey presto, blooming again in the correct direction.

My own little daughter, Amalene, was always terribly ill with chest problems, but she began to get and stay well, and I believe this was another prayer answered so quietly and quickly, for which I thank Jesus.

Around that time, in 1982, another prayer was answered to do with myself and my daughters, Amalene and Shiralee. I prayed that their father, Peter, would someday become a child of God, and out of the blue he mentioned wanting to read the Bible, which was presented to Amalene at a Sunday School.

Then another amazing thing happened. My sister Shirley and my brother Tyrone flew me up to Johannesburg to meet my son Floyd, who was arriving from New Zealand. I was so thankful, as it was a great expense to my son, Floyd, and we got on so well after eleven years of not seeing one another.

Whilst on my vacation, I couldn't manage my sister Shirley's electric kettle, which was not easy to check or refill the water level. I promised myself that when I got back to Durban, I would send her a beautiful whistling kettle. Then, you wouldn't believe what happened. Shirley's housegirl gave her a kettle, just like the one I described, out of the blue and for no reason at all. So you see, the Lord knows what we need before we do.

Another work of the Lord happened while I was reading my Bible one evening (St. John, 6) and my son Floyd was sitting on the other side of the room. As I was reading, I wondered whether or not he had heard the story of the five loaves of bread and two little fishes. Suddenly, on the Christian tape I was playing, which I had borrowed and never heard before, a piece was read from the Bible… and yes, it was loud and clear, all about St. John 6, the five little loaves and two little fishes. So, praise the Lord, I hope my son heard it loud and clear.

Another friend of mine, Gysbert, had returned to Holland but was supposed to be coming back to South Africa again. As the months passed, I suddenly thought about him, when a girl friend of mine, Esme, mentioned seeing him in Durban and that he had lost my address and couldn't contact me.

Before she told me that, I had decided I would try and contact a friend of his, Mary, but I could not remember where she was employed. I was sitting in town one day, waiting for the bus, when I saw the name of the company she worked with. I decided I would call them the following day and ask to speak to her.

The next day I had a doctor's appointment, so the first task on my list after that was to make the telephone call to Mary. On my way home, I stopped at a drive-in restaurant for a milkshake, when I lifted my head and standing just near my table was Gysbert! What a lovely surprise! He told me he was running late, had spoken to Mary early that morning, and was on his way to meet her, but had just stopped off for a cool beverage as it was such a hot day! Isn't it wonderful the way the Lord works?

For some time I'd had a feeling to phone an old friend of mine, Roger, a ship's pilot, who had been very troubled the last time I saw him. When I called him, I was amazed at this new man; he was so at peace. He did not know that I had found the Lord, and I did not know he had either.

At the end of the evening, he said, 'I'm going to tell you something now which will probably bore you—'

I stopped him and said, 'Roger, don't tell me. Let me tell you. You praise the Lord now!'

Oh, it was so wonderful. Amen.

I prayed so much to be able to find a girlfriend that praised the Lord, so that we could do things together, and eventually made friends with Aileen. I had met her on a couple of occasions, not knowing she was a Christian. Discovering that she was made me so happy – another answered prayer.

My Prayer and Poem, also in song
THERE COMES A DAY

There comes a day when things must be done.
There comes a day, when it's almost won.
But the only time is the time you give
To the Lord; I know and that is so.
There comes a day when we need love.
There comes a day when we should give.
And the only way is to pray
To the Lord; I know and that is so.

*Written and composed by Yvonne Woods, 1981*

Since I mentioned the beautiful inspirations the Lord has given me to compose and write music, I have written several other songs: 'Jesus, I Thank Thee', as I feel we have so much to thank him for; 'There Comes A Day', and we have many of those; 'I Am Happy Now', which He has made me; 'It's A Beautiful Day', and we have many beautiful days; 'The Only Way', and I'm sure you will agree with me, He is the only way; 'A Dear, Dear Prayer', well, that is really all we need; 'I Am A Christian', Christians are people who are always happy and have a closer communication with the Lord; 'Just

Reach Out Your Hand', which is so true – he is so close to you; 'Ever To Love Thee', well, that explains itself; 'Take My Heart, Jesus', and how I prayed my heart was good enough for Him to take; 'This Is A Song From The World', to tell Him we need Him, not only when we need rain; and 'I Want To Sing For You, Dear Lord, well, when your heart is happy, you sing. These are all the wonderful inspirations and thoughts He has given me.

My Prayers and Poems in song
A DEAR, DEAR PRAYER

Could you really spare,
A dear, dear prayer?
It's all we really need,
Dear Lord.
Deep within my heart, there is a start
Of a flame that burns for you.
Could you really spare,
A dear, dear prayer?
It's all we really need,
Dear Lord.
So when we pray,
Let it be every day,
So the flame can really burn.
Could you really spare,
A dear, dear prayer?
It's all we really need,
Dear Lord.
Yes, it's all we really need,
Dear Lord.

*Written and composed by Yvonne Woods,1981.*

My Prayers and Poems in song.
I AM A CHRISTIAN

I am a Christian; what is he?
Christians are people who are happy.
We get happy on the spirits of the Lord,
Which gives us the strength to carry on.
We are always ready, to help the blind to see,
The dumb to speak,
And the deaf to hear.
I am a Christian; what is he?
Christians are people who are happy.
We get happy on the spirits of the Lord,
Which gives us the strength to carry on,
We use our eyes for the blind to see,
We use our hands for the dumb to speak,
We use our ears for the deaf to hear,
Not forgetting those who cannot walk,
Which gives us the strength to carry on.
I am a Christian; what is he?
Christians are people who are happy.
We get happy on the spirits of the Lord,
Which gives us the strength to carry on,
Which gives us the strength to carry on.

*Written and composed by Yvonne Woods, 1981*

My Prayers and Poems in song
JUST REACH OUR YOUR HAND

Just reach out your hand,
Looking for the Lord,
Looking for the Lord.

Don't go miles away,
He's not very far,
Looking for the Lord,
Looking for the Lord.
Just reach out your hand,
And you will be glad,
Looking for the Lord,
Looking for the Lord.
You shouldn't have to go very far,
So there you are,
Looking for the Lord,
Looking for the Lord.
Just reach out your hand,
And you will be glad,
Looking for the Lord.

*Written and composed by Yvonne Woods, 1981*

My Prayers and Poems in song
EVER TO LOVE THEE

My joy and my victory,
My Lord and my king,
Ever to love thee,
Ever to sing, anthems of glory,
And praises to thee.
For ever and ever, I will love thee.
The days are so long,
The nights so short,
Thank you, my Lord,
For all you have taught.
Ever to love thee,
Ever to sing, anthems of glory,

And promises to thee.
For ever and ever, I will love thee.

*Written and composed by Yvonne Woods, 1981*

My Prayers and Poems in song
THIS IS A SONG FROM THE WORLD

This is a song, this is a prayer,
From the world. Do you hear?
This is a song, this is a prayer,
To say that we need you,
Not only when we need rain
Again and again.
This is a song, this is a prayer,
From the world. Do you hear?
This is a song, this is a prayer,
Oh, dear God, thank you for being here.
This is a song, this is a prayer,
To tell you we love you, not only in despair.
This is a song, this is a prayer,
Oh, dear God, thank you for being here.
This is a song, this is a prayer,
From the world. Do you hear?
This is a song, this is a prayer,
To say that we need you, not only when we need rain
Again and again.

*All written and composed by Yvonne Woods, 1991-1994.*

Shiralee, my youngest daughter's Prayer and Poem
LOVE, LOVE, LOVE THE LORD

Love, love, love the Lord,
Love, love, love the Lord,
And he will make you happy,
And he will make you good.
Love the Lord and see what he can do for you,
And see what he can do,
And see what he can do,
And see what he can do for you.

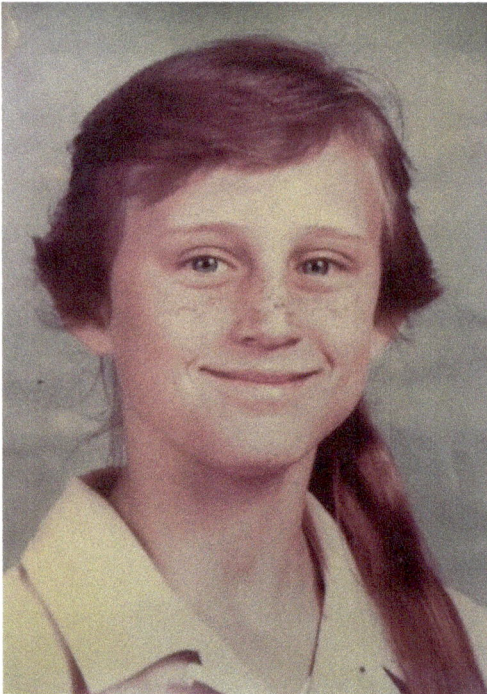

*Shiralee, my youngest daughter, at the age of 10 years, composed 'Love, Love, Love The Lord'*

By this time, my eldest daughter Amalene was also assisting Sunday School, teaching for the Methodist

Church where we worshipped and prayed. Amalene, my eldest daughter, and Shiralee, my youngest daughter, were christened at their own request. After their father's tragic murder, they suggested they could now be baptised, which was so enlightening.

They walked up to the altar with Amalene dressed in white with a red ribbon bow tied around her waist, and Shiralee in white with a pink bow tied around her waist. This was so amazing after not attending church in their younger years. Attending school assembly as they grew older, inspired my daughters to be baptised.

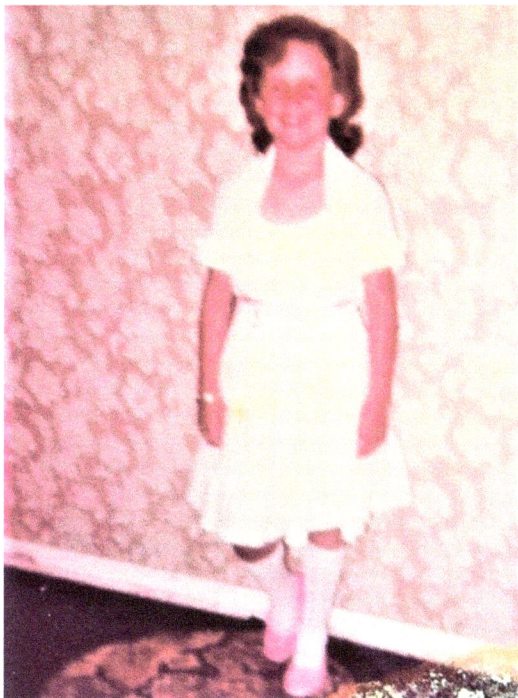

*Shiralee, my youngest daughter, dressed for her christening/baptism, with a pink ribbon*

*Amalene, my eldest daughter, dressed for her christening/baptism, with a red bow*

*Shirene, as seen in her little caged kennel at the
SPCA, awaiting a new adopted family*

Our adopted little ridgeback crossbreed, Shirene, from
the Society for the Prevention of Cruelty to Animals
(SPCA), represented my two daughters' names, Shiralee
and Amalene. Whoever would have thought this
possible! God does work in mysterious ways, Amen.

Shirene was with us during our blessed days of the
girls' baptism, and it was a Godsend to have this
beautiful animal share our love and names.

I was blessed with a godmother, Aunt Kay, my late
father Thomas's sister, but she has since passed on.

I also have a goddaughter, Adele, in South Africa,
who is the daughter of my only brother, Tyrone.

*My late godmother, Aunt Kay*

*My goddaughter, Adele, in South Africa*

*Amalene, my eldest daughter, assisted at
Sunday School in the Methodist Church*

Some may wonder about the words of my song, 'This Is
A Song From The World', when I wrote that we love the
Lord not only when we need rain. But there are so many
times, when we find suddenly there's a world gathering
to pray for all the rain that we haven't had, and the
drought has set in. So, I sing this song and pray to show
that we need Him all the time, not only when we really
need rain.

It is the most wonderful experience to know that without that help from the Lord, you simply would not be able to do something you'd never dreamt or thought of doing, but it just happens as simply and as quickly as that. I just have a thought in my mind about certain people, friends, and family, and the telephone rings and there they are, or a letter arrives from them. This book is my way of sharing the beautiful happenings of the Lord with you all. Can we offer less than our best to God?

Believe me, these experiences are real and true. They have happened to me – an ordinary human being, of flesh and blood, one who never thought of the Lord, never believed in the Lord. And I know I am not dreaming, or taking drugs or alcohol, but truly experiencing the wonderful works of the Lord.

Another experience given to me was when I had for some time felt this inspiration to minister to Fyn, a family friend. I tried to get in touch with him but did not succeed, then his wife Peggy telephoned and I got his number, gave them my thoughts, and prayed that I would be speaking to Fyn soon.

Sitting at the hospital waiting to see my specialist, I started chatting to a little boy who had broken his arm. He had been in a plaster cast for three months, then they replaced his old plaster of Paris cast for a new one. After four months in cast, his flesh had not been damaged in any way and he had no wounds. Children will be children; they are filled with such energy.

Going back to linking this magnificent chain to the Lord, after all these years, I have suddenly come to realise that my brother Tyrone's birthdate, thirteenth

(13<sup>th</sup>) is my lucky number. My English husband Roy is 13 years older than myself.

In another episode about the Lord's chain, my new friend, John, and his sons, Alistair and Robin, all praise the Lord. Well, I was originally married to another John, my son Floyd's father. And this new friend John's son, Robin, has the same name as the Rhodesian Army Medic who saved my life on the roadside after my accident. Through the Lord, I praise Jesus again and again. There is always a long chain linking to God's glory in my life. I know, too, that lightness cannot mix with the darkness.

On several occasions, the Lord has proved to me that He is there, and especially one particular Sunday, when I was truly beside myself and feeling down and just not knowing why. Then suddenly, as quickly as I was feeling down, by reading His word, the Bible, I was lifted right up again. At the same time, I prayed to the Lord and asked Him to please do something small, just to show me He was truly with me. And He did. The day before, I'd had a huge spot or pimple just near the end of my mouth, which I had been pressing and squeezing. Naturally, this meant it grew even bigger. On the Monday, this huge pimple had gone, and that is the first time ever in my life I have been rid of a spot so quickly. It usually takes up to ten days. May I say, this was another answered prayer.

On April 28, 1982, while I was waiting at the outpatients' clinic, I met a gentleman whose name was Ernie. He and his wife, Yvonne, were owners of an estate agency, I also met Ernie's baby. The couple had waited fifteen years for a second child, and their daughter was born on their son's birthday. Her name,

Sharlene, is very similar to my two daughters, Shiralee and Amalene, put together, as is my beautiful little pet/ fury Shirene.

Then in the seat next to me was a Dave. And my stepfather's name was Dave.

After having my x-rays, I was informed of a comfortable new gate to be fitted to my leg, with knee hinges and ankle hinges, then I met the other specialist who measured me up for this plastic fixture, I had noticed a beautiful cross/crucifix around his neck, which I admired it, and I later learned that his name was Mark; my brother Tyrone's son is Mark. In the midst of my conversation mentioning how brave I had become in my life and during which I praised the Lord, he asked me if I was a re-born Christian. I had guessed already, and he revealed that he was, too.

Just ten months after my accident, my supposedly to-be-amputated, squashed, bone-missing, flesh-torn leg with three breaks was well on the mend. I was now putting pressure on it, bending the knee, and moving the ankle. I can only thank Jesus for all the knowledge he has given to our doctors and nursing staff, and the strength, courage, health, painlessness, comfort, and friends for seeing me through such a difficult time. I will always be grateful for the way I recovered and my ability to be patient and calm during that time, as I composed music, wrote songs and took time to look at all sides of the people around me. Without the Lord's wonderful love and help, I would never have made it.

The specialist's receptionist, by the way, knew Ian, the driver of the motorcycle accident, through Hobbiecat sailing. I hope this long chain, which links friends and me to the Lord, will never end.

The Lord came to my rescue again on another occasion when I was baking a birthday cake for my daughter, Shiralee, who was about to turn eight years of age. We had decided on a house-style cake but, not being in my own home, had to make do with whatever utensils were available in the kitchen. The square pans were rather huge, so I looked at the deep, round-shaped ones and decided on making a rondaval (an African house made in South Africa) cake. Only the Lord could have done this for me.

The cake had to have the shape of a round, pointed roof, as that is how the South Africans, or Zulus, built their homes. Both my daughters, Amalene and Shiralee, helped me with the baking of the cake, but at that stage we had only used two baking dishes. I was wondering whether or not to do a third layer, so as to get the height for the pointed roof top, when suddenly, in the last five minutes of cooking, one layer started to rise to a point in the middle of the baking dish. It was absolutely marvellous. God is marvellous, because the other layer had baked perfectly flat, so all we had to do to the cake was put one layer on top of the other, then ice and decorate. And it turned out to be fantastic. I could never have managed it without our Heavenly Father.

Still testing the Lord, I decided to make another cake with the same recipe some weeks later, to see if I had perhaps done something wrong to make the rondaval cake turn out that way. But this time, the cake was flat and round, as all cakes should be.

In another tremendous way of the Lord, I met a gentleman, Magnus, whom I joined to attend an engagement-cum-birthday party for my ex-colleague,

Anne, only to find that Magnus had a son, Greg (my baby sister's son is also named Greg), who was studying in the ministry with the Baptist Church. I was praising the Lord and speaking of my wonderful encounters, when Magnus mentioned that I should attend their Baptist worship. A week later, I was asked to sing my songs for the Lord at a house meeting in Umhlanga Rocks, for the Baptist Church, and this all took place through my physiotherapist, who is a Christian. I am certain by now, my friends, that it is possible to see that Jesus is here and does see us, and he certainly answers our prayers.

Something else that just happened was when I was thinking about my friend Lawrence, who I mentioned earlier in the book. Anyway, he telephoned me within days of him going through my mind, and on impulse he drove out to see me from Durban to Umdloti. He presented me with a tiny blue elephant, which reminded me of my first present in hospital, after my motorcycle accident. My daughters, Amalene and Shiralee, presented me with a beautiful pink elephant to keep by my side and look after me. So now I had pink and blue elephants to keep by my side and look after me.

Another prayer of mine which was answered was how I longed to meet a friend in Umdloti, close to my home. Lo and behold, I met Jack, who had been on his own for seven years. But unfortunately this gentleman was completely the opposite to me, and not at all interested in my relationship with my Heavenly Father.

However, another friend, Magnus, was brought into my life. He attended the House of the Lord and we shared the same interests. He had two wonderful sons, Gregory, who was to go into the Ministry, and Jeffrey, serving in the Police Force. As we all know, we are given a will of our own and I knew the Lord was testing me. So, although I had prayed for a friend near home, I had also prayed for a friend to join me in the House of the Lord. Of course, I chose my friend Magnus, but at the same time I remembered Jack in my prayers.

*My baby sister, Jeanette, prayed, 'Please, Jesus, let my car start.'*

I always included my baby sister, Jeanette, in my prayers, but one time I had a wonderful inspiration. As I could not afford to purchase her a gift whilst she was put to bed by doctor's orders, I decided to continue painting a verse from the Bible in the colours to match her bedroom – purple. It read, 'All things whatsoever ye shall ask in prayer, believing, ye, shall receive. Mathew 21, verse 22'. I thought it would probably be pushed into some drawers, or a cupboard.

However, a couple of weeks went by, and in another beautiful happening, the Lord showed my baby sister what He can do. Their car had been delivered to them some weeks back and was left on the front lawn, unable to start. It had lain for so long that it was terribly dirty and weathered, so Jeannette thought she would put it away in the garage. What even gave her the thought, she didn't quite know.

She got into the car and, before doing anything, she prayed to Jesus, 'Please, Jesus, let my car start.' And when the engine suddenly started into life, she could not believe it! She was so shocked!

When her husband, Godfrey, got home, he was absolutely amazed that the car had been moved and asked Jeanette if she had pushed that heavy vehicle. When she told him the story, he was stunned and said, 'Well that is a miracle!' Only a few months before, he had been questioning my religious attitude, and saying I was a religious freak!

The Lord answers all prayers sooner or later – but in his own time, so don't rush him. Just thank him. Their little son Barney announced that he would like to go to church to thank Jesus for helping his mommy. Praise the Lord. Unfortunately, he missed the bus, but, was informed that he could still thank Jesus right there in his own home!

I stopped writing and taking note of all these miraculous happenings for several years, and did not put pen to paper again until October 1988. But the

Lord had been good to me throughout, and I had been offered my old job at R.M.S Syfrets, Durban, where it all happened for me when I became saved through a voice on the other end of the telephone line (Rufus's voice).

May I share with you all that a lot happened in-between all these years. One day, I was flat broke, really penniless, having had quite a few heavy expenses. I hadn't purchased my weekly bus coupon and couldn't, because as I only had five Rand (R5.00) on me and my bus coupon cost me 16 Rand per week (South African currency).

However, I duly handed the bus driver my five Rand note, when he handed it back to me and said, 'I do not have any change.' At the end of the journey, I again handed the bus driver the money. Well, it was hilarious, as the driver had no intention of taking my money, but at the same time he didn't want all the passengers to see what was going on. Praise God for the driver, who did not know my financial position at all.

In another mention for the work of the Lord, my excellent orthopaedic surgeon remarked that it was 'a miraculous healing' that I could walk tall without any limp or evidence of having almost had my leg amputated. I was left with a very slight scar, but could wear my stiletto heels without any problem at all. Praise God. In return for all the surgeon's healing hours devoted to me, I sent his wife a thank you gift of porcelain flowers, which she happily accepted, Unbeknown to me she loved pottery, in appreciation of her patience and understanding and being there for my specialist! Unbeknown to me, she loved pottery.

A Poem written by my attorney, Mr. Van Der Merwe, in 1981
INTO INFINITY

Imagine, a love, above,
The spaces of the universe.
Larger than life,
Beyond infinity.
Imagine a vastness,
A beingness,
Which contains all,
In tender serenity.
Imagine understanding,
Beyond forgiving,
A divine love that,
Extends above,
Any love, that's ever
Been known.
And you will know,
That one supreme,
The one that will redeem,
And grant life,
And lovingness,
Once again,
Towards a new beginning,
Of greatness and fulfilment
Of being, doing or,
Loving in all universes,
Into infinity,
Into the love of him,
Supreme,
And thus be, divine again,
And thus be divine again.

*Written for Yvonne Woods.*

A very sad moment was when I heard on the United States of America news that a former American Idol contestant by the name of Jennifer Hudson sadly lost a great part of her family. My heart broke for the singer, and somehow I composed a lyric for her.

I couldn't quite make up my mind as to which was the best lyric title.

## IT'S HARD OUT THERE – GOD, BE MY BODYGUARD

It's so hard out there,
God, be my bodyguard.
The chores of life,
The jaws of life,
It's so hard out there,
God, be my bodyguard.

I need to dance,
I need to sing,
It's so hard out there,
God, be my bodyguard.

The ups and downs,
The ins and outs,
It's so hard out there,
God, be my bodyguard.

Family and friends,
All other ends,
It's so hard out there.

When your heart's burning,
And yearning and yearning,

It's so hard out there,
God, be my bodyguard.

A broken heart, tears you apart.
It's so hard out there,
God, be my bodyguard,

Jack of all trades,
Fender benders,
It's so hard out there,
God, be my bodyguard.

The past blasts,
Present upheavals,
It's so hard out there,
God, be my bodyguard.

Sweltering sun, pouring rain,
Oh God, here comes the hail,
It's so hard out there,
God, be my bodyguard.

Dogs running wild,
Cattle enjoying the crops,
It's raining cats and dogs,
It's so hard out there,
God, be my bodyguard.

*Lyrics written by Yvonne Woods, 2008*

Unfortunately, I have not persevered in presenting my lyrics to Jennifer Hudson. My prayers for her healing and many blessings.

God's love is so real, so powerful, so overwhelming. He loves me, He loves you, and He can fill our lives with His love, and we can say 'I love God', and to those around you, 'I love you'.

It is now the year 2020 – a very confusing, difficult year of the Covid-19 pandemic, lockdowns, face masks, staying at home, no shopping for the elderly or people with underlying medical conditions, tracing and tracking each contact; all part of trying to curb the virus. And the whole world has been affected.

*Me wearing my compulsory face mask during the Covid-19 pandemic*

Many families and friends have lost their lives in this terrible time. May they all Rest In Peace. Although there have been so many sad moments for the world, we have used our God-given brains to act wisely, cautiously, and lovingly for all the people.

Vaccines have now been developed by large pharmaceutical companies, as many put their thoughts and expertise together to try and find a safe way to save families from the dreaded virus. Praise the Lord for our God-given brains.

*My prayers for the world: Stay safe 2020*

Praise God, my first book, *Bits And Pieces Of Evita's True Life Story*, was published in the year of 2020 – 39 years after I wrote it. I was truly blessed to have had the inspiration to write my true-life stories and find I am still amazed at having done so. I just know it was a God-sent inspiration.

It has been asked, 'Well, why do we have all our ups and downs? Why does God allow suffering?' (Romans, 5:12, and Peter, 3:9) People seem to feel life should be full of joy, with no worries or woes.

In my life, there has been heartache and pain, but we have a God-given brain and we must use it to meet our Heavenly Father halfway. Life is what we make it, but also what others make it for you. Compromise is another good step in life, as is learning by our mistakes. Amen! With positivity comes faith, hope, love, and comfort.

I always look at life as in a flower – it grows, then it goes off. Or like a car where the vehicle's parts eventually wear down. We humans have to join our maker sooner or later.

The Only Remedy is an inscription from the Woman's Auxiliary meetings leader Ruth at the Methodist Church in Durban:

'Since the most basic fact about man is that he is a sinner, his most desperate need is for a Saviour. Nothing else and nobody else will do. Let him go to a psychiatrist, and what does he become? An adjusted sinner. If he goes to a physician, he becomes a healthy sinner. If he achieves wealth, he becomes a wealthy sinner. And if he joins a church and tries to improve himself by merely turning over a new leaf, he becomes a religious sinner.

But let him go in sincere repentance to the foot of the cross and accept the finished work of Christ for himself, and he becomes a new creature with new meaning and purpose in his life and the peace and joy of the Lord in his heart.'

I must tell you about another unbelievable happening, which occurred since my first book was published in 2020. My late mother, Elizabeth, was given for her 80th birthday in 1999, a beautiful present of a gorgeous pair of pink silk pyjamas from her granddaughter, Amalene. I inherited these pyjamas from my mother and have worn them many times. They are still in my wardrobe

But it was only in September 2020 that I noticed the label on the pyjamas is 'Success Story', and I only discovered this after my own success story was published. And, strangely, I have never in my lifetime seen or heard of any clothing labels with this mark.

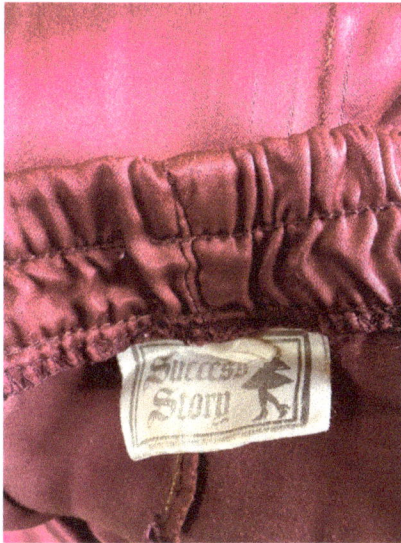

*My mother Elizabeth's pink silk pyjamas labelled 'Success Story'*

These very same beautiful pink silk pyjamas were also the cause of my lovely elderly neighbour Doreen writing and composing a special relevant poem for me.

It all began as I waved my husband Roy goodbye one morning, and the front door slammed shut. I was locked out of my home, standing in my late mother's pink silk pyjamas, and had to chase down the street after my husband to retrieve his house key.

*My lovely elderly neighbour Doreen, who wrote a special poem dedicated to me*

## A TRUE WINTER'S TALE

Evita saw Roy on his way,
It was time to start the day.
The Christmas decorations, though,
From the porch should come down now.
As she reached to take them down,
The door banged shut; she was alone.

Pink pyjamas, slippered feet,
Out she ran into the street.
Long hair flowing out behind
As she ran, blown by the wind.

'Darling, Darling!', filled the air,
She could see Roy way up there,
Along the road, the distance fair,
But, alas, he couldn't hear.

'Darling!' rang out yet again
As she called him, all in vain.
Roy was walking way ahead
But at last, he turned his head.
When he saw her —'What on earth!'
Was torn between concern and mirth.

His dear wife out in night array,
Her silken night clothes on display.
*(If she'd worn a flimsy nightie*
T'would be worse, and far more draughty.

Key obtained and safely home,
She put on clothes and hair did comb.

Now she makes sure that a key
Will on her person always be.

On reflection, what a feast,
And for Simpson Road a treat!
How she laughs now at the way
Her silky pinks went on display.

*Written and composed by my elderly neighbour Doreen for me in 2019*

As the years have gone by, I have always been interested in reading horoscopes as a way of checking to see how the verdicts relate to my family. So recently I came across my granddaughter Storm's star sign. Part of the inscription said 'take a break'. And amazingly, part of my *Bits And Pieces Of Evita's True Life Story* was to be featuring in the magazine *Take A Break*, on the 10th September, 2020!

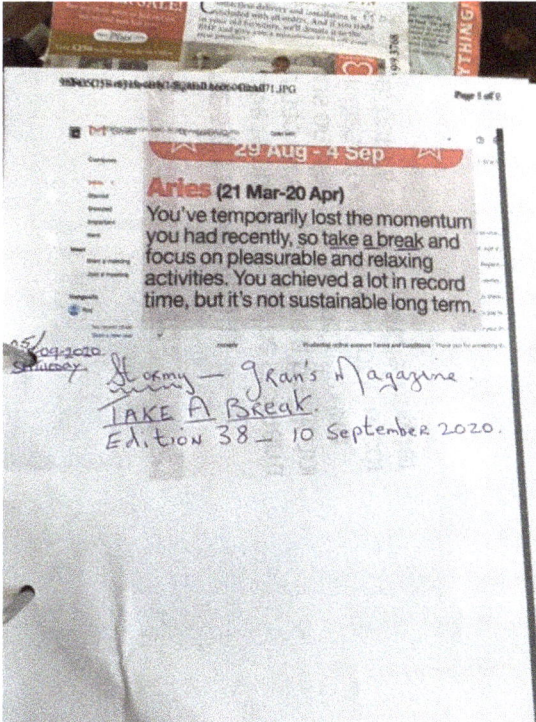

*My granddaughter Storm's horoscope mentioned 'take a break' – the magazine I featured in*

In another most wonderful happening, I have recently been blessed to be told by my cousin Marilyn, who resides in Canada, that my Aunt Patricia is resident here in Bath, UK. I have been a resident in the United Kingdom, for the past nine years, but 62 years have been lost between us. What makes it even harder to accept is the fact that this Covid-19 pandemic doesn't allow any visits, but thankfully, through the expertise of modern technology, we can at least be in contact throughout the days.

*My cousin Marilyn in Canada*

*My Aunt Patricia, in her good young nineties, lives in Bath.*

Aunty Pat purchased my first published book "Bits and Pieces of Evita's True Life Story" and said "is was the highlight of her day, when reading it daily".

I lost my late father, Thomas, in 1958, when I was almost 17 years old. I also then lost contact with my Aunt Patricia, through moving on and moving away.

So, finding out she was living in the same country as me was an absolute Godsend. She is now in her good young nineties, and I am so blessed and truly thankful to receive this news and for us to be in contact again.

Once again, I need to stress that these coincidences are definitely true blessings from God, not coincidental, all true happenings. Amen!

Sadly, I must add at this point that I have been diagnosed with Dementia – an incurable brain disease – but I feel so blessed that I have been able to use my brain to highlight, explain, and possibly prove that there is more to one's life than they think. We need, faith, hope, love, one another. Memories and miracles do happen. Thank you, Jesus.

*My pens presented to me during the process of writing*
*Bits and Pieces of Evita's True Life Story.*

I would like to pinpoint another unusual happening. As I look out of my big glass sliding doors, I see so many wonderful moments. One day, as I was gazing, there was a young couple on a long narrowboat, moored on the Grand Union Canal right alongside my doors. Many boats moor outside my home, and I wave and greet them often. But for some reason I decided to go outside and speak to the young couple.

When I introduced myself as Evita, the young girl responded, 'Hi, I'm Ava.' I picked up a foreign accent, which I remarked on, and asked where she originated from. It turned out Ava was Italian, which brought to mind my wonderful Italian former neighbours in Rhodesia/Zimbabwe in the 1970s, who were from Sicily. Ava said she came from Venice, which jogged my mind that my eldest grandson, Jarryd, had recently visited that beautiful city Venice and enjoyed the pleasure of a Gondola boat ride.

*My eldest grandson Jarryd in Venice on a gondola*

The conversation also brought back to mind the daughter of another ex-neighbour, here in the UK, who was called Ava.

*My late mother would talk of going to Remania –
to remain here!*

I then asked where Ava's partner was from and she said, 'Romania. His name is Daniel.'

That made me smile, as it brought back a childhood memory of something my mother would say. We siblings would ask here, 'Where are you going, Mommy?' and her response was, 'To Romania.' In other words, 'To remain here.'

This lovely young girl Ava and I had a good laugh about that when I related the story from my youth.

Although my mother's name was Elizabeth, most times she was referred to as Betty. So that is where Betty-boo, my eldest daughter Amalene's beautiful little breed-cross Lakeland Terrier's name comes from. There's always something there to remind me!

*Betty-boo, my eldest daughter Amalene's dog, always brings to mind my mother*

Just recently (2019), I was in a cafeteria when I was served by a lady from Romania. How absurd is that! Again, I related the 'Remain here' story, and a good laugh was had by all.

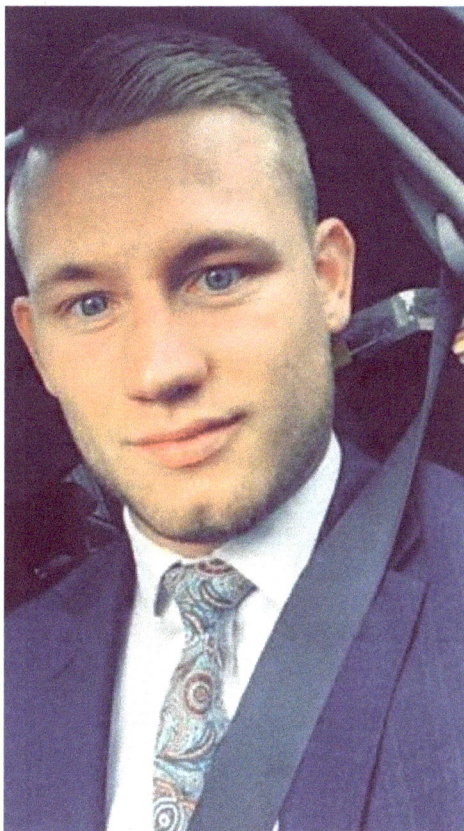

My second eldest grandson, Clyv (CJ).

Anyway, the boy on the boat's name also rang a few bells for me. My second eldest grandson, Clyv's (CJ) partner is named Daniella. And when I mentioned this, there seemed to be no end to all the various links, as Ava said, 'That's my sister's name, Daniella.' Absolutely unbelievable.

*Daniella, my grandson Clyv's partner in New Zealand*

*Evita's eldest grandson Jarryd's partner, Jasmine,
who resides in New Zealand*

Mentioning my second eldest grandson Clyv's (CJ) partner brings to my mind a very good South African friend Helga, who resides in Australia. Her eldest daughter's name is Jasmine, and my eldest grandson Jarryd's partner is also named Jasmine. The long chain in my Heavenly link never ends.

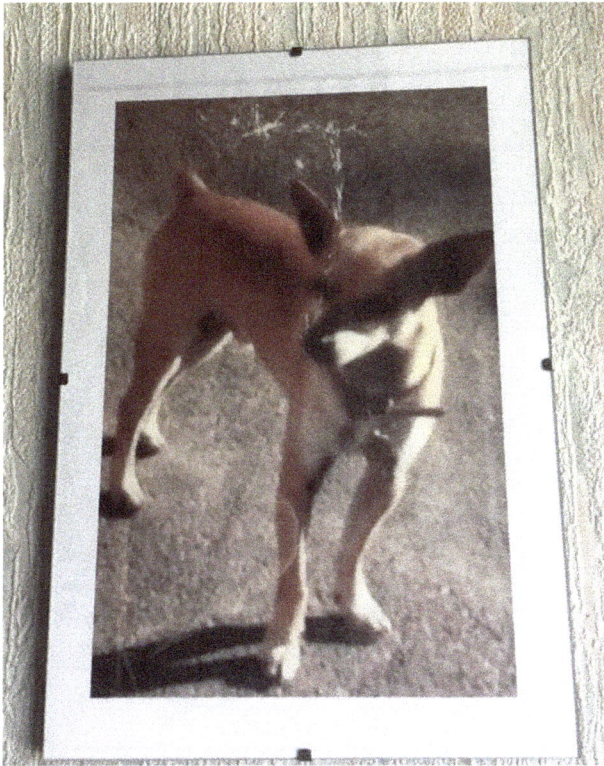

*My beautiful Milo was a sweet Min Pinscher dog breed*

That same South African friend, Helga also owns a magnificent Bull Terrier breed named Milo. And my own beautiful Milo was a sweet little Min Pinscher dog.

*My English husband Roy's nephew, Paul*

Sometime during the year 2019, my English husband Roy and I had lunch out with his lovely nephew Paul and his good friend Tom, his lovely sister Ann and her husband John, from Canada. We ate in a little pub in Crawley. Funnily enough, Crawley was my name for a while, after one of my previous weddings. And what should I find on the lunch table but a beautiful table coaster with a picture of two lovely horses, which actually resemble my daughter Amalene and my granddaughter Storm's horses, Bertie and Domino.

*The table coasters resemble Bertie and Domino,*
*our family's horses*

It's amazing all these wonderful happenings and connections in my life.

*My eldest daughter Amalene with Domino, and my granddaughter Storm with Bertie*

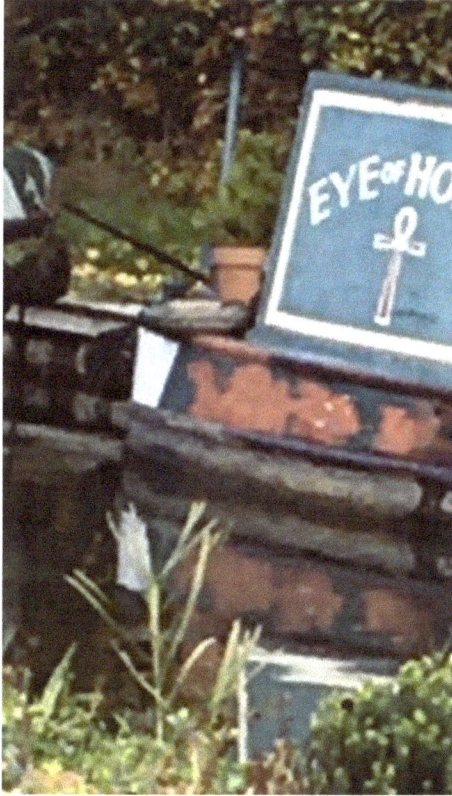

*EVITA YVONNE ELIZABETH: E.Y.E. moored outside
my glass sliding doors*

As I was just about to finish writing about all these
so-called happenings, I suddenly noticed outside my big
glass sliding doors a long narrow boat moored with my
initials E.Y.E. alongside a beautiful religious cross.

I just had the inspiration once more to have a little
conversation with the boat owner, so I introduced
myself and explained that those were my initials. He
explained that he was called Horus, and that the full

name of the moored boat was *E.Y.E. of HORUS*. Isn't that a wonderful coincidence? There is a little more to what meets the EYE!

Another one of my blessings is that my middle name is Elizabeth, as is Her Majesty Queen Elizabeth II. I have become a British Citizen and feel so privileged to be in the United Kingdom, under the reign of Her Majesty Queen Elizabeth II. My late mother was blessed with the name Elizabeth, and likewise I blessed my two daughters Amalene Elizabeth and Shiralee Elizabeth, and my granddaughter is Storm Elizabeth. And these names were all chosen long before we contemplated migrating to the United Kingdom.

*This long narrow boat, Wandering Star, reminded me of the song by Lee Marvin*

When the time came for the long narrow boat named *E.Y.E.* to move on, it was soon replaced by another one, named *Wandering Star* – and I just love that song sung by Lee Marvin. After humming and hawing, I eventually called out to the boat owner, who also had a darling pet whose name was Boson. But I mentioned my sentiments to him, only to find that he was really a wandering star and never ceased to walk here, there, and everywhere with his beloved Boson, who he said gave all the orders!!

The song brings to light the song I often sing to console myself over the loss of my late daughter, Rene Pearl, out at sea in New Zealand It's called 'They Needed A New Star Up Yonder', and mentions that God decided he would send for 'a star and so he sent for that little kid sister of mine'.

Not only do I have a wonderful view of boats, but I often see some lovely pets walking with their owners. Another long narrow boat moored nearby had a fabulous ginger kitty, and they are my absolute favourite I didn't have the pleasure of taking a photograph or the name of the ginger kitty, but it did bring to mind Furby, my granddaughter Storm's ginger furry. Amazing.

*Furby, a Devon Rex breed, my granddaughter Storm's furry*

Furby, a Devon Rex breed, has a lovely ginger tinge to her beautiful tight fur. She loves drinking running water, so has a water fountain feature to drink from. Furby belongs to my granddaughter Storm, here in the United Kingdom.

*My brother Tyrone's pet French Poodle, named Scruffy*

I could not go another day without remembering Scruffy, a beautiful French Poodle in South Africa who has passed away. It broke my heart, but at least I have fond memories and had the honour of a cuddle.

Unfortunately, the ginger kitty Scruffy – a Ragdoll cross Manx cross breed, born no tail – is in Australia, but I have been blessed with seeing his photographs.

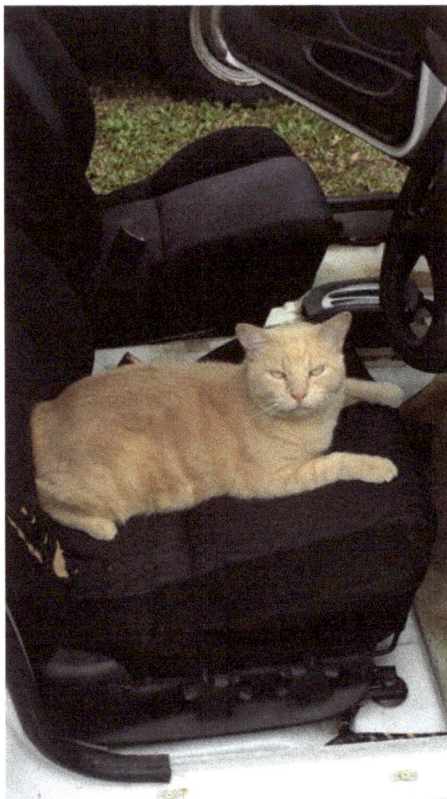

*Scruffy, my son Floyd's pet in Australia*

Unfortunately, they say that 'all good things come to an end', but I also maintain that all good things 'come to those who wait' and that patience is a virtue'. I still have many more years to live and I cannot simply see the end to all my God-given beautiful experiences, but I need to end my story by wishing all my family, inherited families, adopted families, friends, Facebook contacts, WhatsApp contacts, Messenger and Instagram contacts – just too many to name – *au revoir*, goodbye,

God Bless, and tell them 'never, never, never give up. The Lord is great.' Amen.

Perhaps somehow, sometime, somewhere, or even someone shall be able to enlighten me of all these coincidental happenings, as I have another happening.

My very good friend in South Africa, Trixie, has a beautiful great granddaughter Eva, whose mother is Candice. And my beautiful great-granddaughter Leah's mother is also named Candice.

*My good family friend Trixie, who sadly passed away 2020. May she Rest In Peace.*

*My inherited grandson Tomas always brings to mind my late father Thomas. May he Rest in Peace.*

In recent times, I inherited a grandson, Tomas, whose father's name is Dave. Coincidentally, again, my late father's name was Thomas and my late stepfather's name was Dave. May they both Rest in Peace.

Now some more unreal blissful links with my family's beautiful pets. Bentley, a breed-cross Teacup Yorkie Bichon and Shitzu, lives in style with a Bentley parked in the driveway of their home – the vehicle owner being David, who as I have said brings to mind my late stepfather David.

*Bentley – the cross-Teacup Yorkie Bichon and Shitzu, my eldest daughter Amalene's beautiful pet/furry*

And it doesn't end there. My neighbours, Jeannette and Peter, live up the road from my new home in the United Kingdom, and thinking of them always brings to mind my late husband Peter (may he Rest In Peace), and my baby sister Jeanette, who is a resident in Vanderbijlpark, South Africa.

On top of all these happenings, my granddaughter Storm just got married in 2019. As I had my late husband's nephew, Thomas, visiting from South Africa, the family were taking outdoor photographs, when suddenly a boat moored just behind me with the name

*Peter*. Of course, that was my late husband's name, my granddaughter Storm's late grandfather's name! It was amazing, as though he was taking part in the wedding blessings. Surely everyone must now believe there is a God out there. He must be looking over me.

Peter long narrow boat moored on
the day of the wedding 2019

Having mentioned my late husband Peter, his nephew Thomas in South Africa brings to my mind again my late father Thomas.

*My granddaughter Storm's Protea South
African flower centre designed bouquet*

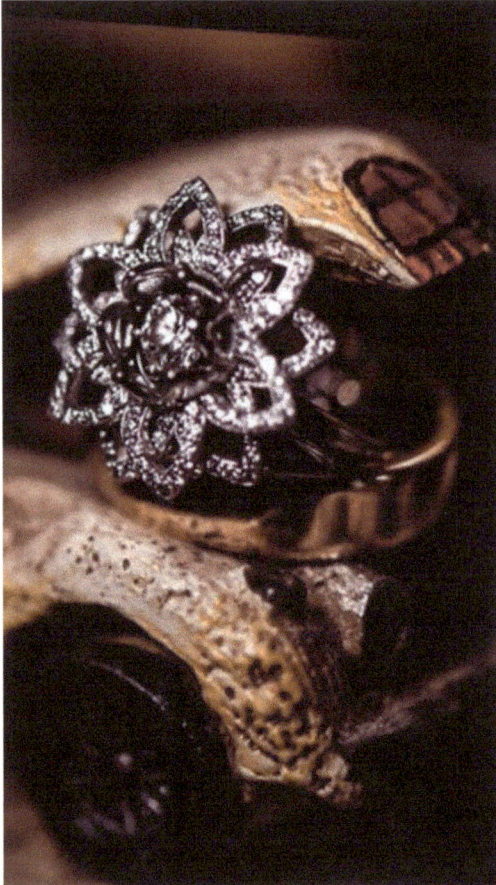

*My granddaughter Storm's Protea South
African flower centre designed ring*

*Long narrow boat named Protea sailing by during
the wedding events in 2019*

*Penny Flight, a long narrow boat sailing by (long reeds blocking the full name) during the wedding events in 2019*

This was another fantastic happening or Godsend, when a long narrow boat named *Protea* sailed by on the day of the wedding. This was amazing, as my granddaughter Storm had her bridal bouquet made up as a Protea – a South African flower – and her wedding rings were also made up to represent the South African bloom!

Please, believe me, the next long narrow boat that sailed by was named *Penny Flight*, and my granddaughter Storm is employed as crew on British Airways flights She also has her private pilot's licence. What a Godsend!

Penny Flight *long narrow boat sailed by during the wedding, and my granddaughter is in the flight business. Another Godsend.*

*I am still in* AWE! *What a Godsend.*

*Storm, my granddaughter's wedding gown,
designed by Maggie Sottero*

Maggie, *the long narrow boat sailed by. Another blessing!*

The next long narrow boat was *Maggie*, and my granddaughter's wedding gown designer was Maggie Sottero. Also, her late great-great-grandmother was known as Maggie. And that is not all! A long narrow boat named *Storm* also sailed by. It's unbelievable. And this all happened within June, July 2019, when the wedding was held. I am certain these were very Godly blessings from our Heavenly Father.

Storm *long narrow boat also sailed by*

*I share my birthday with my English husband Roy, in the first week of December*

I now need to say my English husband Roy and I have birthdays in the same week of December, but even more importantly, I share the exact same day – December 4 – with his late mother, Josephine. May she Rest In Peace. It is so sad that I never met her, but I am so blessed that she gave birth to such a wonderful son, Roy, who asked for my hand in marriage in the year 2011.

*My husband Roy's mother, Josephine, photographed in
1945/6, was born on December 4, like me*

My husband Roy's late Granddad Joseph, 1899/1901.
May he Rest In Peace.

I do believe that life was prepared for me even before I was born. Yes, before my birth. It is said our lives are planned for us, and I believe that.

I have now learned that my English husband Roy's Granddad, Joseph, was in South Africa in1899/1901, during the Boer War. I migrated to South Africa many years later and lived half my life there, treading the same soil of South Africa as Joseph had done. Then I migrated to the United Kingdom and was married in 2011 to Roy. Now there is not only Joseph the Granddad, but Joseph his middle brother, who is now my brother-in-law. The heavenly inspirations and happenings just never end. Such Heavenly links.

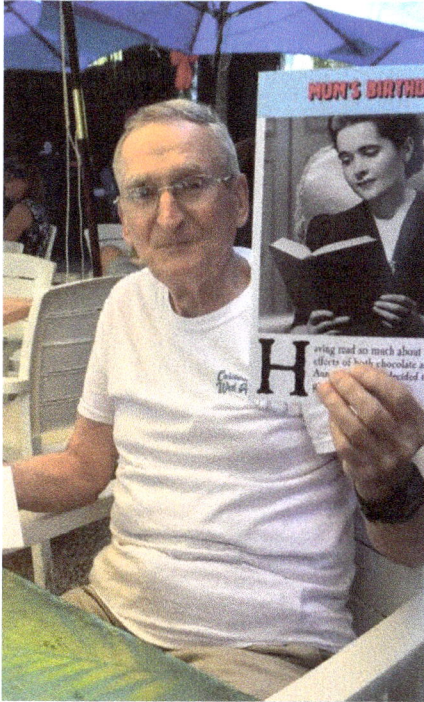

*Roy's middle brother Joseph holding up a birthday card for their late mother Josephine, whose 4th December birthday I share.*

I am still in absolute awe that my husband Roy's niece, his youngest brother David's daughter Megan, shares her birthday with my eldest daughter Amalene on the 30th May. It is another absolute miracle that I should have so many links and blessings with my new family in the United Kingdom. How and why has all this happened in my life? I say it's incredible; a Godsend.

*My husband Roy's niece Megan shares her birthday
with my eldest daughter Amalene*

*My eldest daughter Amalene shares her
birthday with Megan*

I have an inherited adopted granddaughter Lisa, who resides in Sweden, and believe it or not her birthday is on the exact same day – 8$^{th}$ December – as my husband Roy.

And Roy's son Malcolm has his birthday on the 1$^{st}$ December – the exact same day as my cousin Donna-Jane, who resides in South Africa. One has to believe that there is more to this than what meets one's eyes.

*My husband Roy's nephew Stephen*

To top it all off, my husband Roy's nephew Stephen has his birthday in the month of February, and my youngest daughter Shiralee and son-in-law Simon's wedding anniversary is in the month of February. Just too many coincidences.

*My cousin Donna-Jane, who lives in South Africa, shares a birthday on 1st December with my husband's only son, Malcolm*

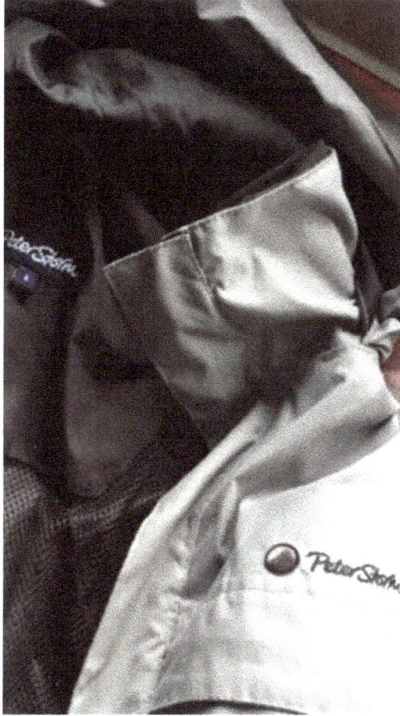

*My husband Roy's rain jacket – by Peter Storm, designer*

Another incident drawn to my attention just recently was that my English husband owns a rain jacket, labelled Peter Storm, which he has had for many years. Now, Peter was my late husband and Storm is my granddaughter! There is so much to remind me that it seems as though, somehow, we must have been connected years back.

I just love Nando, Skylah and Kaydon's beautiful Cavachon breed, which is a designer breed between King Charles Cavalier and a Bichon Frise fury. And, I just love Nando's chicken!

My very good South African friend and former neighbour, Sharon, who resides now in the United Kingdom, has a brother Brett. He lives in the UK and owns a doggy farm. His sister has been blessed with the same name as my cousin Sharon who resides in South Africa, and owns her own Doggy Parlour. I refer to the two ladies – Sharon my cousin, and Sharon my good neighbourly friend – as Shaz and Shazzy. That is unbelievable.

Brett has been blessed with a gorgeous son named Cody. Now Cody, the new baby son, brings to mind my good neighbour Gloria, who lives just up the road in our neighbourhood, and has a gorgeous pet dog called Cody.

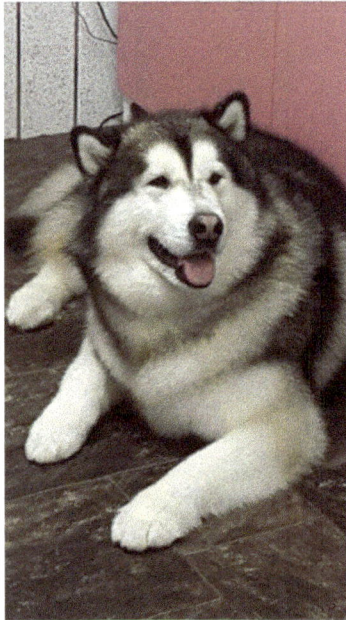

*Cody has the same name as the new baby son on the doggy farm*

My good neighbour, Gloria, who lives just up the road from me, has a gorgeous doggy named Cody. He is a pure breed Alaskan Malamute, registered with the Kennel Club, and his breed name is Samjoe Lone Bear after a Native Indian Chief of America. Cody is walked and always beautifully groomed by Dan, Gloria's tall, slim son.

Cody is a very special name in my heart and my good family friends Brett, Yalda-Efe-Hira, Ralph, Jason, Sharon, Les, and the late Nola, all from the Doggy Farm here in the United Kingdom.

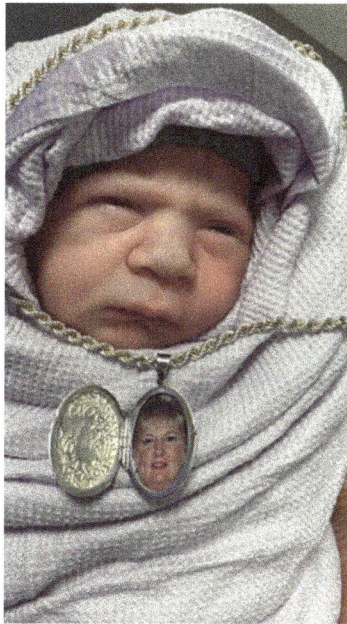

*My late friend Nola's grandson, Cody, adorned with his grandmother's locket, Nola. May she Rest In Peace.*

My good friend, Nola, had recently migrated to the United Kingdom from South Africa. She adored her little doggy on her son Brett's doggy farm, named Cody. And her little grandson was named after his Nola's doggy on the farm. Sadly, Nola passed away in 2020, shortly before her grandson Cody was born.

I have had the honour of knowing Nola's family for many years, but just recently, through the modern technology of Facebook, I met Diane, who lives in New Zealand. She refers to my late friend as Mom Nola, and Diane shares the same name as one of my really beautiful aunts. Many Heavenly links.

*Diane in New Zealand befriended me through Facebook.*

I also have family resident in New Zealand: Simon, my son-in-law; Shiralee, my youngest daughter; my four grandsons, Jarryd, Clyv, Austin, and Trystin; and Leah, my great-granddaughter.

My inherited grandchildren here in the UK – Mitchell, Zoe, and Logan – have an adorable little dog, called Charlie. And I have had the pleasure of holding this loveable pet. He brings to my mind my good former neighbour in South Africa, Leanne who is now resident in Canada. Her family had a beautiful Cockatiel named Charlie, and all I ever heard him sing was 'Charlie, Charlie, Charlie'. He could also mimic the ringing telephone and had me running many a time from my pool to answer the phone when we were neighbours in South Africa.

Having brought to mind all the dogs and the birds, the name also reminds of my favourite fragrance, Charlie. 'Always something there to remind me', as the song goes! And the array of the perfume lingers on.

*Me and Charlie, a Cockapoo*

I had the pleasure of holding Charlie, a Cockapoo crossed Poodle and Spaniel breed, at a fabulous family Christmas party hosted by Chantal and Neal for their family – parents Yvonne and Edward, brother Clinton, sister-in-law Kim, and my inherited new grandchildren, Mitchel, Zoe, and Logan, who own the lovely Charlie. He is very spoilt and has a lovely family who take him for his daily walks.

*Evita and Nando, Cavachon designer breed*

I also have visits from Nando, the Cavachon designer breed who belongs to my inherited family in the United

Kingdom. Neal, Chantal, Skylah, and Kaydon all spoil the beautiful Nando with lovely walks and doggy toys.

*Winston, a Chorkey- Chihuahua-Yorkshire Terrier*

And not forgetting the beautiful, handsome Winston – a Chorkey/Chihuahua/Yorkshire Terrier. His family – Neal, Chantal, Kaydon, and Skylah – love spoiling him with lovely Christmas presents and walks along the pathways.

And Winston brings to my mind the super commemorative coins which are engraved 'Never, Never, Never give up', by Sir Winston Leonard Spencer

Churchill – a previous United Kingdom Prime Minister. To my absolute delight, my one and only brother Tyrone shares one of Sir Winston Churchill's Christian names – Spencer. Hallelujah, Amazing Grace!

*My coin collection includes this commemorative coin with Sir Winston Churchill*

I'm certain most people have heard of the delicious Nando's, with its delicious chicken. And the beautiful dog, Nando, always reminds me of the Nando's delicious meals when I hear his name. When do all these coincidental, inspirational happenings and God-sent reminders and links end?

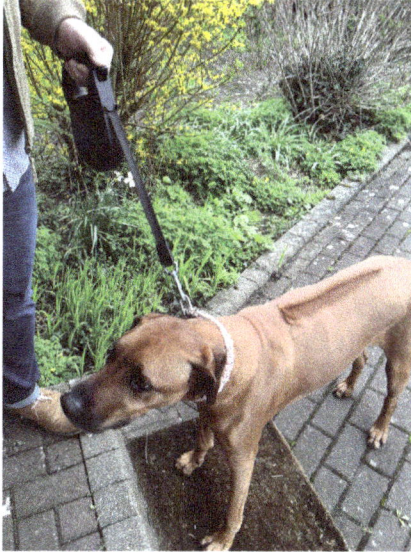

*I beckoned the strangers over to my home so I could admire their Rhodesian Ridgeback. Rhodesia was my birthplace, although it is now named Zimbabwe.*

Can anyone imagine how or why I should suddenly have had my attention drawn across the street from my home, where a couple of people were walking their large brown dog, with the most gorgeous ridge along the top of his back. It was a Rhodesian Ridgeback, and I was absolutely stunned as Rhodesia/Zimbabwe was my birthplace. Not only that, but as a youngster I had never really had any dealings with the Rhodesian Ridgeback breed. I called out to the strangers and beckoned them over to my home, where I could admire their beautiful pet.

*My English husband Roy and his youngest brother David*

My husband Roy's youngest brother David shares the same birthday 13th July with my only brother Tyrone, who resides in South Africa. Now number 13 has always been my lucky number and likewise my husband Roy, who is 13 years older than me.

David has the same name as my eldest daughter Amalene's partner, and also my late second stepfather, may he Rest In Peace.

My eldest daughter's partner David has a son named Tomas, the same name as my late father Thomas, may he Rest In Peace.

My husband's son, Malcolm, here in the United Kingdom, shares his birthday with my cousin Donna-Jane in South Africa, on the 1st December. This is so amazing, and I know they all have the same love for our Heavenly Father. Praise The Lord, many Blessings.

*My cousin Mary-Anne, who resides in Zimbabwe,*
*a born-again Christian*

The latest happening or Godsend I have recently experienced, I have only just now related to a cousin of mine who resides in Zimbabwe. MaryAnne is also a born-again Christian, and her reaction was, 'It was Heaven you saw!'

I have not mentioned this for fear of being told I am hallucinating, and although I have been diagnosed with Dementia, I am still very aware of my surroundings.

As far as my diagnosis is concerned, I compare it to an old vehicle whose parts have worn down, and believe you me, my brain has been stretched over the course of my lifetime. I still have the blessings of being able to accept the things in life one cannot change. Life goes on.

*Life Goes On – this long narrow boat sailed by. Amen.*

It was early morning and I cannot say if I opened my eyes or whether my eyes were still closed, but I had a strange sensation. As I lay on my back in bed, I saw up on the ceiling a beautiful pale blue sky – yes, sky – with hundreds of teeny, weeny stars glittering. It was beautiful. Then I felt as though I was peeping through my half-opened eyes, and didn't want to have a good look as I was a little afraid of what was going on. It was early morning, almost time to rise.

Even I am finding it difficult to believe, but I know it did happen! Mary-Anne, my cousin, said she believed it was Heaven I saw.

It is now forty years ago since I had my huge motorcycle accident, and to date I still am pain-free. I walk in high/stiletto heels with no limp, which is such a God's blessing. Amen.

I began my second job with a panel beating company owner named Roy, in Rhodesia/Zimbabwe, 1958. And today I am married to an Englishman called Roy, here in the United Kingdom, 2020.

upright bushy varieties Evita

Evita

*My upright bushy fuchsia variety*

Ending my wonderful blessed moments, another wonderful experience happened to me since I married my English husband Roy. One day, a beautiful gardening pamphlet appeared through the letterbox, and imagine my absolute surprise when I opened it up and saw Upright Bushy Varieties Evita Fuchsias.

I now actually own three pot plants of Evita's Fuchsias and they have constantly bloomed. I have named each petal with my four children's names: Floyd, the late Rene, Amalene, and Shiralee. It's unreal to find my namesake Fuchsias. It's another Godsend.

I know I am still awaiting a long narrow boat to sail by called *Evita*, but you know patience is a virtue, and with all my life experiences, I know that whatever shall be will be!! Amen.

*Poppy, the beautiful and gentle West Highland Terrier, brings so many blessings and reminders of the wonderful red poppy blooms*

In all my years of living in various countries, I have never had the beautiful red poppy flower growing in my garden — until I came to the UK.

They grow in many gardens here, and we see so many people wearing the poppy on their lapels to represent Remembrance Day.

This all came to mind when I had a lovely cuddle with Poppy, the beautiful West Highland Terrier owned by my niece Jacqueline, Neil her hubby, and my two great nieces, Amy and Catherine, who live here in the UK.

It brought back memories of the fallen, and how so many beautiful red poppies are laid in wreaths to represent all who fell fighting for our country.

Amongst all our beauty, God made animals, flowers, friends, and family, and we have so much to be grateful and to thank Him for.

Life goes on!

*My visit to Dubai to see family resident there*

Visiting Dubai was another one of the most beautiful God-sent happenings in my life. I never in my wildest dreams had ever contemplated travelling there, but as coincidences have it, I had the wonderful occasion to visit my family who are resident there.

My youngest sister Jeanette's eldest son Barney and daughter-in-law Lyudmyla live there and her youngest son Gregory, daughter-in-law Ghie, eldest grandson Jayden, and youngest grandson Joshua. And my sister-in-law has her young son Stephen, Alexandria her daughter-in-law, Finlay her eldest grandson, and Lilly youngest granddaughter there, too. Who in their wildest dreams would ever have thought I would be there? AMEN, AMEN.

*Life goes on. I laid a wreath for my late daughter Rene, who was lost out at sea in 1979, at Wangamatah, New Zealand.*

This book highlights my personal experiences and true happenings, not coincidences, which have given me much food for thought. And I pray my story will give others the same understanding as I have witnessed!

I have always maintained that our Heavenly Father reaches out to others, through one another. He knows our every need, if it is good for you!

Remember that 'Patience is a Virtue'.

And the sooner we go on our knees, AMEN, AMEN, the better!

www.ingramcontent.com/pod-product-compliance
Lightning Source LLC
Chambersburg PA
CBHW050822090426

42738CB00020B/3456